LINCOLN CHRISTIAN COLLEGE AND SEMINARY

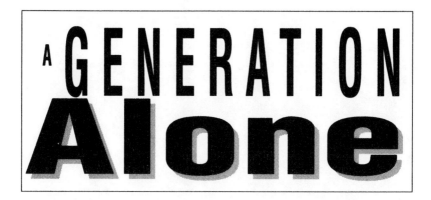

A GENERATION Alone

Xers Making a Place in the World

WILLIAM MAHEDY & JANET BERNARDI

INTERVARSITY PRESS
DOWNERS GROVE, ILLINOIS 60515

InterVarsity Press® is the book-publishing division of InterVarsity Christian Fellowship®, a student movement active on campus at hundreds of universities, colleges and schools of nursing in the United States of America, and a member movement of the International Fellowship of Evangelical Students. For information about local and regional activities, write Public Relations Dept., InterVarsity Christian Fellowship, 6400 Schroeder Rd., P.O. Box 7895, Madison, WI 53707-7895.

Scripture quotations, unless otherwise noted, are from the New Revised Standard Version of the Bible, copyright 1989 by the Division of Christian Education of the National Council of the Churches of Christ in the U.S.A., and are used by permission.

Cover photograph: Michael Goss

ISBN 0-8308-1696-8

Printed in the United States of America

Library of Congress Cataloging-in-Publication Data

Mahedy, William P., 1936-
   A generation alone: Xers making a place in the world/William
Mahedy and Janet Bernardi.
     p.   cm.
   Includes bibliographical references.
   ISBN 0-8308-1696-8
   1. Generation X—Religious life.   2. Generation X—Conduct of
life.   I. Bernardi, Janet, 1968-   .   II. Title.
BV4529.2.M34   1994
248.8'4—dc20   94-18634
                                                          CIP

17	16	15	14	13	12	11	10	9	8	7	6	5	4	3	2	1
08	07	06	05	04	03	02	01	00	99	98	97	96	95	94		

With much love and great respect
we dedicate this book
to the members of our
Young Adult Community

Acknowledgments

We are very grateful to Rodney Clapp, our book editor, for his suggestions, his careful editing of our work and his encouragement. We thank Chris Nichols, the San Diego director of InterVarsity Christian Fellowship, for his insistence that we write this book. We are most grateful to those young adults of our own community, of the salons and of other campus fellowships who consented to be interviewed. Their stories and insights are integral to the book. We express our thanks and affection to the members of InterVarsity Christian Fellowship and the other Christian fellowships who have been so important to us. Finally, we are grateful beyond words to the members of our own Young Adult Community. This book is the result of our life with them.

Introduction

Generation X: A View from the Inside (Janet)

In May 1989, thousands of Chinese college students waged a massive peaceful protest in Beijing's Tiananmen Square. They were campaigning for freedom from their tyrannical government. On my college campus in California we watched with immense pride and admiration as people our age worked together to change their world. Most of us did not regularly watch the news, but during those weeks we followed every detail as the square filled with more and more students and the military finally moved in. We cheered and wept for joy at seeing a single student stop a line of tanks. We wanted so much for their movement to succeed. Then we watched in horror as the protestors' own government fired on them and set their bodies ablaze. That week many of us wore black armbands handed out by the Chinese Student Association. At our campus and across America, students held candlelight vigils in remembrance of the slain students in China. We knew without a doubt if we had been Chinese, we too would have sat in that square.

A couple of weeks later, during our Homecoming week, a riot broke out on campus. Roughly a thousand students from my campus and other local schools moved in a mob through the college part of town, breaking windows, burning cars, looting the liquor store, beating each other up. They had no real purpose for rioting. There was no cause, nothing significant to protest, not one thing to justify their actions.

While our brothers and sisters were marching in Prague, Lithuania and China to protest their lack of freedom, American students, drunk on their own freedom and driven by an underlying boredom, cursed the police and each other, flagrantly daring the world to subdue them.

I was furious at the misguided zeal and destructiveness of my fellow students. I knew what really drove them was anger at their own irrelevance and disgust at the lack of anything vital in their lives. Nothing in America seemed important to them—that was the root of their anger. Their emotional outburst masked their apathy.

But I realized the source of their energy. Their feelings were also mine. Like me, many of them wished they could have been in Tiananmen Square during May 1989. I and others my age wanted desperately to make a difference in the world; we wanted nothing more than for our actions to have some meaning. It was then that I realized the immensity of my generation's restlessness.

My generation has been called various things by our elders, not many of them positive. We have been described as lazy, useless, ill-educated and shallow. We are considered a Peter Pan generation, unwilling to grow up, slow to start careers and launch families. We are defined in contrast to the generation that immediately preceded us— and that likes us least—the Baby Boomers. In their eyes they are the world's boom and we its bust. Thus we are called the "Baby Busters." We have also been called "Generation X" because it was thought that we stand for nothing and believe in nothing.

Being born in the 1960s makes me a member of Generation X. Like all of us born between 1961 and 1981, I am an "Xer." This Xer graduated from college in 1990, joined a throng of recent graduates backpacking in Europe, then moved back in with parents while searching for a job. I found employment, moved to San Diego, and discovered—as so many Xers have—that my degree (a bachelor of science in biochemistry) was good for a job that paid not much more than the minimum wage. I was appalled to discover that I was competing for such entry-level positions with people who had ten years' or more experience.

Douglas Coupland, himself an Xer, published a book that he called *Generation X.* After I read it, I invited some friends to discuss it in a salon-style group once a week. I began to visit coffeehouses and talk to people I met there about our generational issues. I even carried on conversations with other Xers on computer bulletin boards. I was amazed to discover that the restlessness and anger I sensed in myself were to be found in every Xer I encountered.

Then I began working with Bill Mahedy in campus ministry, and we continued researching this phenomenon together. In our study of Generation X we have uncovered some startling, disturbing facts. We have discovered the impact of anomie—the lack of moral standards in society—on my generation.

Xers' generational experience has taught us things about the harshness of life and the need for change that the rest of the world is only now beginning to realize. Bill and I are encouraged by what we have discovered about my generation's strengths and willingness to start off in new directions. We believe that despite our generational weaknesses—perhaps *because of* them—Generation X is nothing less than the harbinger of a brighter future.

On the Outside Looking In (Bill)

I remember well my first meeting with Janet. It was a new school year. Our campus ministry had planned what I thought was a good Bible study series, but for the second consecutive Sunday evening, several potential student leaders didn't show up. As the college chaplain I had put some effort into planning the series, and I was concerned. I called one of the students, who told me that my potential leaders had all been at Janet Bernardi's house at *her* Bible study.

"Who," I asked, "is Janet Bernardi?"

"She's awesome," was the reply. "We met her on the retreat weekend up in Los Angeles a couple of weeks ago. She's just out of college herself, she lives in San Diego, and she offered to have Bible studies for us in her home."

More than a little annoyed, I obtained a phone number and called this person who had intruded into my campus-ministry pastoral turf, conducting Bible studies with who knew what kind of training or background. We arranged a breakfast meeting at which I intended to deliver a lecture on the seriousness of Bible study and the need for proper training.

The lecture was never delivered. Janet introduced herself, we ordered breakfast, and she told me about her long involvement with InterVarsity Christian Fellowship, her experience as a Bible study leader, her commitment to her parish church and her desire to do ministry. Clearly I was in the presence of an enthusiastic, very intelligent young Christian who loved the Lord, so I invited her to work with me in campus and young adult ministry as my assistant. She accepted, and thus began a most fruitful collaboration. Now, almost two years later, I never refer to Janet as my assistant but as my associate, coworker and friend.

One thing I discovered very soon is that Janet is at least as hardheaded and stubborn as I am. Neither of us can persuade the other of anything without facts and convincing arguments. At first I thought she was overdoing it with her emphasis on the unique problems of Generation X, but she pointed out something we had both observed: younger college students seemed to have more problems than those of the very recent past. She explained that they were more "brittle," and for some very good reasons that had to do with rapidly accelerating family breakdown, loss of hope and economic stress. I had already realized this, but Janet put a name to it and forced me to focus on the problem.

Janet told me of her "salons for twentysomethings," her discussions with other Xers in coffeehouses, and the many ways she had been conducting informal research. She had inquired among a wide variety of friends and acquaintances—fellow Christians, agnostics and unbelievers. Her questions covered the entire range of life: political, economic, social, moral and religious. I was impressed, but still skeptical, so I embarked on my own research.

When we first met, Janet had been out of college for about a year and I had been a campus pastor for ten years. For more than ten years prior to coming on campus, I had in succession served as an army chaplain with a tour in Vietnam and then as a Veterans Administration social worker. During that period I worked mostly with soldiers and with Vietnam veterans. Most recently I had been a cofounder and designer of the nationwide Vet Center Program; I'd been a Vet Center counselor, serving veterans who had suffered the terrible emotional and spiritual wounds of war.

The Vietnam War and its aftermath had influenced my perspective, especially as I'd had to confront the presence of real evil. For some months before meeting Janet, I had entertained the rather disturbing thought that working with college students was beginning to resemble working with veterans who had been traumatized by war, but I hadn't worked through the implications of this. I began to do so through Janet's "crash course in Generation X" and through my own observations and my work in campus ministry. Pieces of the picture began to fit into place, and I had to agree that Xers were indeed different from their predecessors.

Not content with either Janet's observations or my own, I began to interview other campus pastors, InterVarsity leaders, clergy, teachers, medical and mental health professionals—my contacts are extensive and include people from all parts of the country. There was general agreement that the spiritual and psychological problems of young adults and teenagers were far worse than those people had encountered in preceding generations.

It seemed that Janet was correct in her assessment of the problems, but was her insistence on the strengths of her generation also on target? My work with college students and other young adults convinces me that she is correct there as well.

In our joint ministry, Janet's role is to act among her peers as a member of the community, but increasingly as a leader, while mine is to provide the usual pastoral support of the clergy. In our discussions—most of them still at breakfast meetings—Janet brings her own experience of life as a well-trained and deeply Christian member of Generation X. I bring a longer life experience—thirty-two years longer—and I connect her insights with biblical and classic Christian theology. From these discussions grew the idea for this book.

We intend the book primarily for members of Generation X, for theirs is the deepest spiritual need. We want to help Xers understand more fully the challenges they face in a world that increasingly withholds nurture from its young. Above all we want to share with them the promise of the gospel and the One who transforms lives and allows us to change the course of history—even in times as troubled as our own.

But the book is also for parents, teachers and anyone interested in this new "lost generation," so that they might be better able to provide the support and nurture that are essential to young adults.

And we envision another readership as well. During the past year or so, we have discovered people of all ages who are experiencing a disillusionment with life not unlike the lack of hope with which many Xers begin young adulthood. So the book is intended for these "honorary members" of Generation X, those who have begun to notice society's crumbling and are looking for new hope.

Finally, we are aware that the world is entering a new era that will be defined by major cultural shifts and moral and religious confusion—and it is a world dominated by technology. We hope this book will, in a small way, break some new ground for a theology of the twenty-first century, the time in which Generation X will come into its full maturity.

As the book unfolds, we will compare Generation X with its predecessors. We will make comparisons between Xers traumatized by life in America and veterans traumatized by war. We will explore the search for meaning and God. We will discuss healing, personal relationships, the church and how to live in society. We will end with a personal spirituality that we believe is appropriate to Generation X—and to those who would be serious Christians in the emerging world.

Janet's role in the book is to lead, to articulate the Xer's point of view—religious as well as secular—from within the generation. My role is to check out her observations with my own, to test her perspective against the longer view, to connect it with history, Scripture and traditional theology.

Throughout the book we retain our two distinctive voices. We believe this is important because of the differences between us. Janet is twenty-five years old, female, unmarried and embarked on a career. She is a member of the Church as a layperson. I am fifty-seven years old, male, married, the father of two children. I am ordained to the pastoral ministry of the Church.

Interestingly, we are two generations apart. This is another reason for maintaining distinct voices. Janet is an Xer; I am a member of the "Silent" generation. The Boomers lie between us. Boomers are for Janet, as for many Xers, a kind of nemesis. For me they are former students, fellow soldiers and veterans—not bad youngsters in my view, but tending to be spoiled and somewhat self-righteous. I mention this because we will discuss the Boomers, we hope with fairness and objectivity. Boomers receive special mention because they play such a large role in the life of Generation X.

The final reason for maintaining our distinct voices is simply because we are both too hard-headed to have it any other way. Janet is not willing to let me speak for her; I am likewise unwilling to let her speak for me. This is as it should be. If, as I believe, older generations must above all nurture and guide the young, this is not done except by listening to and then challenging them. Only when they speak to us as equals have we fulfilled our responsibilities to them. Only then can we feel comfortable in leaving to them both the world and the Church. They in turn must learn from us something of the wisdom of age, of Scripture, theology, history, of faith and of what life is all about. Only then are they ready to assume the responsibility for the world and the Church.

My work with young adults—and my collaboration with Janet—has convinced me that within Generation X are some of the finest Christians I have ever encountered. I have no fear of a future in which they will lead. The Spirit is as much at work in this generation as in any in the past.

So we invite you, the reader, to listen to our distinct voices, for we hope we have reached a harmony of openness to the Spirit. We invite you to join us, two friends in Christ, as we seek to discern how the Spirit is moving among us at the threshold of a new century, especially among those who are now young adults but who will largely determine the shape of that century.

1
ALONENESS

How Is the World Different for Xers? (Janet)

Often it is difficult to explain myself when I say, "Things are different for my generation." Every young person since the beginning of time has had the same complaint. When I point out that we are surrounded by violence, I am reminded that there has always been violence in America—consider the Mafia. When I try to explain how poor the job market is now, my grandparents, who lived through the Great Depression, say I do not know what a poor job market really is. But even people of my grandparents' era will admit there is *something* different about youth today.

In order to understand what that "something different" is, we must look at the way today's youth—Generation X—are united by some disturbing facts. Over half of us have divorced parents. More than half had working mothers. We were the first generation of "latchkey" kids. An overwhelming number of us (one in three) were physically or sexually abused, often by a stepparent. Many of us were neglected by well-meaning parents in pursuit of their careers.

Among twentysomethings a college education is assumed and required for a career position. Women of our generation are expected to go to college, earn degrees and pursue careers alongside men. It was not so for my mother. This increase in education has enabled tremendous leaps in technological fields. Ironically, technology has enabled uneducated workers to perform tasks previously reserved for highly educated ones. Technology also makes possible massive layoffs in the work force. In a large sense an entire generation has been or can be replaced by technology.

Aside from the technological advances, women and men of my generation have witnessed tens of thousands of murders on television and movie screens. To us, sex on TV and safe-sex commercials are routine. We matured faster than our predecessors due to advances in health care, but we are marrying later and having children later.

We were born in the Nixon era and have never known national trust in leadership. In fact, we have seen corrupt leadership in everything from PTL Ministries to the Los Angeles Police Department.

Xers and Boomers

This is the first time ever in the United States that one generation will have a lower standard of living than their parents. Among Xers that fact has fostered both frustration and a surprising sense of relief, for we tend to look upon the conspicuous-consumer Boomers with disgust. Perhaps there is some underlying envy because the Boomers happened to be at the right economic place at the right time, but there is more to it than that. The standard of the "good life," that which has been accepted as the new norm, has been raised so high that in families both spouses are now required to work at paying jobs. Generation X knows what this means in terms of diminished parental involvement. We Xers have paid the emotional price for the consumer society in which our elders have participated so fervently.

Our generational priorities have shifted out of economic necessity—but even more out of a powerful desire to have in adulthood what
we lacked growing up. We do not need a BMW. We do not need a
summer cottage. We do not need tailor-made clothes. What we do
need and want is a cohesive family unit!

Yet we are torn, ambivalent. We find ourselves again and again
trying to live up to what the yuppie generation say is necessary. They
define success by people's salary, car, home, clothes, where they vacation and where they send their children to school. They judge
people by how successful their careers are. A successful career has
become synonymous with a successful person. This leads men and
women alike to put all their energy into the furtherance of their
careers.

Xers have been roundly criticized for not following this trend, for
not pursuing careers with a similar vengeance. Our priorities, they say,
are backwards and twisted. The truth of the matter is that we started
in the direction the Boomers pointed and quickly saw that it was
pointless. We Xers are reluctant to embark on the same path as the
generation before us. Career is a yuppie notion. Before careers came
into vogue, people worked simply to support their families, not to gain
their life's fulfillment. They had more free time, and they raised their
own children. Xers wonder aloud who have their priorities straight.

These are some of the facts that unite us as Xers. We have many
things in common with the generations preceding us. Rebellion
against the status quo, for example, is the norm for youth. But what
is the source of our difference? Where does the apathy come from?
Whence the distrust? The restlessness? The lack of commitment? Why
do people of my generation, knowing the outcome, still wish they
could have been in Tiananmen Square?

Alone in the World

I think what defines us as a generation is "aloneness." Let me begin
with a story. Not long ago, I found a friend crying because her brother

had failed to fulfill a promise—again. She was devastated by the realization that she had never been able to rely on him, or on anyone. My friend, like many Xers, learned very early to rely only on herself. She felt abandoned by her father, who had left after her parents' divorce. She felt abandoned by her mother, who had pursued her career and left her with a nanny. And she felt she could never rely on her brother, who was following well the examples his parents had set. She felt alone.

Though a story like this could be told about individuals in any generation, the situation is so common among Xers that it has become the norm. Many, perhaps most, of us have never experienced real reliability and responsibility. My friend cannot rely on her family for support—nor can she rely on her mechanic to be honest, her doctor to prescribe only the tests that are necessary, her friends to help bear her burdens, or strangers to be kind. She feels afraid of being shot, afraid of being held up at the cash machine, afraid to go alone on a date with a man. Like many Xers her age, she is financially independent and lives with roommates. But no one really needs her, and she needs no one. This is aloneness.

My friend is like many of us. We've been raised to think only of ourselves—we've been raised by the "me generation." We were *told* to think only of ourselves, so we *had to* think only of ourselves. No one else thought about us. We raised ourselves. We couldn't really trust anyone.

Aloneness is being alone and not being able to trust anyone. It carries over from family life and friendships onto the job. My own job situation is fairly typical. I am expected to be there, but I am not really *needed*. This was made very clear to me recently when one of my coworkers, who has about the same training and experience as I, was replaced by an eighteen-year-old high-school graduate—who can be paid less. Like many people my age, I work at a job where I could be easily replaced. We know that no one really needs us. We could disappear and nothing would change.

Again, this experience is not entirely unique to the last twenty years, but it has become so commonplace that it is characteristic of Generation X. We are like random molecules bumping into other molecules.

Aloneness is not loneliness. While loneliness is a state of emptiness, in aloneness one's life is full of activities but without the aid of family or friends. It encompasses a basic distrust of people and a fear of being hurt. Aloneness is largely about fear. It stems from abandonment or neglect and leads to alienation from friends, family and society. Aloneness is a survival technique and comes across as independence. Aloneness separates this generation from every other.

Because of the direction society has taken, other generations are now beginning to experience widespread aloneness. We Xers, however, grew up with it, so perhaps we can not only discover a way out of it but explore the richness and spiritual depth that one can find in being alone.

Discovering Generation X (Bill)

Janet's paradigm shift in understanding her generation, the "aha!" moment when she saw things clearly, took place during the 1989 turmoil in China and the reaction to it on her college campus. Mine was more gradual but occurred about the same time. During the early and mid eighties I was aware that students hadn't changed much since my own college years in the fifties, nor did they differ greatly from the students I had taught in high school and college during the sixties. During my early years in campus ministry, students would come into my office for spiritual guidance, for counseling or just to talk. They were not haunted by images of death and destruction as were the veterans with whom I had worked for so many years. Their enthusiasm for life was undimmed by cynicism and nihilism. They had problems with studies, doubts regarding faith, religious questions. They were trying on their newfound independence, sorting out relationships with parents, dating and searching for potential life partners— doing the same things my generation and my former students had done in college.

That was in the early eighties. But as the decade waned I began to notice significant changes in young adults. They were, I suddenly noticed, more traumatized by life. They seemed more isolated and alone, more fragile. Hope for the future seemed diminished.

I remember the first time I allowed myself the thought that working with college students was almost like being back in the Vet Center. During the closing session of a weekend retreat with about sixty young adults, a woman in her early twenties admitted that she had very little to live for and had contemplated suicide. Others nodded in recognition of her anguish, and the floodgates opened as people poured out their pain. A fellow retreat leader, also a man of middle years, later remarked to me, "It used to take sixty years to build up this kind of trauma, but now they do it in twenty."

Not long afterward, our young adult group did a Bible study on Galatians 6:2: "Bear one another's burdens, and in this way you will fulfill the law of Christ." The questions for discussion were "What are your own burdens?" and "What are the burdens of others?" The outpouring in response was intense: people listed sexual abuse, drug-addicted and alcoholic parents, mothers and fathers who really didn't care, the pointlessness of life, the meaninglessness of education, a future with little more than low-paying jobs. I was deeply troubled to discover that these were the realities of life for my young friends.

The Aberrant Becomes Normal

I was aware, of course, that older generations had confronted similar problems. The difference was that dysfunctionality and trauma had never before been the *prevailing* conditions for most American youngsters. What had once been considered unusual or aberrant behavior now seemed to have become the norm. At some point society's treatment of the young had shifted from nurture to hostility. My dawning awareness of this change was the beginning of my own "aha!" moment. Janet talks about how shell-shocked and battle-weary her generation feels. Can it be that members of Generation X resemble survivors of combat? Can it be that simply being young in America can create attitudes and problems that resemble service in a war zone?

I voiced this question to mental health professionals around the country who were friends from my Vet Center days. These were acknowledged experts in treating war-related stress, and they thought my comparison had some merit. I learned from talking to them that the younger the age cohort, the more serious the trauma and dysfunction and the higher the percentage of those afflicted.

Because of my work with Vietnam veterans, I am frequently invited to participate in classes and training sessions for teachers, mental health professionals and trauma counselors; many of these are national gatherings. Whenever I report my findings and conclusions about young people, I encounter only agreement and more "horror stories." A university psychologist told me that the pathology among students was "off the scale." A high-school teacher remarked, "There is simply no moral compass." A sixth-grade teacher warned me, "Wait till you see what you'll be getting in college in a few years."

Another similarity between today's young people and Vietnam veterans is their relationship to religious faith and the search for meaning. For many soldiers, the war experience shattered their hope of finding any ultimate meaning or of discovering the presence of God in their lives.

War is the intentional, systematic, institutionalized killing of people. It dehumanizes and brutalizes all who engage in it. The purpose of combat is to kill enemy soldiers. The so-called collateral damage of war is the slaughter of the civilian population as well. Soldiers who engage in war must unleash the most brutish forces resident within the soul. In order to survive, they must undergo a numbing of the spirit. War condemns the soldier to a future of emotional disorders and to a life of cynicism if not nihilism. The spiritual reality of war is stated most eloquently in the one-liner uttered so often by Vietnam soldiers: "It don't mean nothin'." For countless soldiers, God was lost in Vietnam, and with God any religious faith.

For many within Generation X, religious faith is also deformed because of the traumas they have experienced early in life and because of what they see around them now. Campus pastors and many parish youth workers have learned to assume that students cannot hear a religious message free of distortions. For many Xers, God is not a serious concern. Students seem to have developed some kind of grid that distorts traditional Christian language and images of God. Many of them, for example, because of their shattered self-esteem, understand *sin* and *guilt* not in their classical biblical sense but as a personal judgment on them by others.

One campus pastor from the evangelical tradition has discovered a way to deal with this. He never uses the word *sin* in his sermons without clarifying that sin is a form of deliberate selfishness and not a sense of personal worthlessness. By so doing he preaches the gospel effectively and in a way Xers can understand, but he also avoids the pitfall of psychologizing the faith.

Janet once used the word *brittle* to describe many in her generation. The word is appropriate and all-encompassing, denoting both the emotional insecurity rampant among the young and their fragile hold on the legacy that is normally bequeathed to each generation by those who precede them. The legacy given to them, in any case, is materially diminished, spiritually impoverished and reluctantly given. The bumper sticker conveys quite accurately what we are doing in every way to our young: "We're spending our children's inheritance." We are spending it not only economically but morally and spiritually as well. That young people are brittle is entirely understandable. They have been given nothing to support them.

Young adults now joke about a "midlife crisis" at twenty-five. They confide to Janet through conversations on computer bulletin boards that they have already suffered "nervous breakdowns." Life is indeed, as one high-school senior put it, "like my computer. It beeps at me whenever I slip up."

Generation X has been spiritually starved, emotionally traumatized, educationally deprived, condemned to a bleak economic future and robbed of the hope that should characterize youth. Let's look in greater depth at Vietnam veterans to shed light on some of Generation X's spiritual and emotional dilemmas.

Survivors of Combat, Survivors of Life

The fragile relationship of both Vietnam vets and Generation X to their society results from events that by their very nature engulf and disorient the individual. In both cases the wider reality of the world simply overcomes a person's capacity to cope. Such events usually result in serious moral and religious questions and exert a significant psychological impact. The psychological or emotional influences are readily acknowledged in our "psychologized" society. The role of religion and morality, on the other hand, is often overlooked or denied.

In discussing psychological issues of young adults I do not suggest that most are eligible for a clinical diagnosis of any kind. But the population segment that exhibits some clinical symptoms is so large that it affects the rest of the generation, the younger teenage cohorts more severely than the older twentysomethings. Many who have not been traumatized in one way (through parental divorce, for example) have been in another (perhaps through sexual or psychological abuse). Even those who have suffered no serious personal trauma must learn to deal daily with those who have—for they begin to see through a distorted prism as well.

The primary psychological residue of war among veterans of Vietnam and other wars is called posttraumatic stress disorder (PTSD).[1] Very simply, this is an enduring condition that results from a stressful incident beyond the normal range of human experiences (combat, terrorism, genocide, torture, rape, violence, devastating natural disasters).

When a person is threatened with physical harm or psychic disintegration, the only business at hand is survival. Disastrous events generate their own overpowering emotional responses: sorrow, grief, guilt, anger. These emotions are entirely appropriate, but to allow them to surface during the crisis would be dangerous to life, well-being and sanity. The only option is to bury them deeply.

Yet repressed emotions of this intensity always resurface in one form or another and always cause trouble. Dreams, flashbacks, sleep disorders, violent behavior, depression, emotional numbing, feelings of detachment from others and inability to have loving feelings are some of the symptoms. An inability to feel emotion (called psychic numbing) is a root symptom of PTSD.

PTSD can affect individuals, large segments of a people and even entire populations. The Los Angeles riots and the Florida hurricane of 1992 are known to have caused widespread PTSD. I visited Russia in 1988 to work with veterans of the war in Afghanistan; their symptoms were identical to those of American Vietnam veterans. A Russian army psychiatrist told our group that the people of Leningrad (now St. Petersburg) who are old enough to have survived the World War II siege of that city—a siege in which almost a million people died—continue to suffer from PTSD.

Countless young people were psychologically or sexually abused as children, and a great many young women have been raped. Growing numbers of youth are exposed to gang violence and random drive-by shootings in our cities. These young people live in a real war zone. Many of them suffer from clinical PTSD and may require therapy. But the nonclinical "symptoms" arising from unresolved moral, religious and philosophical questions must also be addressed. These are as real as any clinically diagnosable disorder and are often just as devastating—even to the point of causing psychic numbing. My own observations and Janet's confirm this. It is even a matter for discussion among twentysomethings on the computer bulletin board.

Questions of Meaning

Posttraumatic stress almost always raises questions of meaning. Even natural disasters raise moral and religious issues: "Why did God allow this?" "What did I do to deserve this?" In the case of rape or sexual abuse, the questions are even more intense and are usually accompanied by shame and anger. The personal issues arising from these experiences are primarily moral and religious.

Events powerful enough to cause severe PTSD bring about an alteration in consciousness, a new awareness of reality. One's relationships to other people, to nature and to God are seen as somehow changed. Evil becomes real and very personal. The youthful illusion of omnipotence is shattered, and one's vulnerability becomes a permanent feature of consciousness. Life can never be what it was before the event. There is no going back, because truth can never be unlearned—only denied.

This altered consciousness often accompanies clinical symptoms of PTSD but is also found frequently in those with no symptoms. It generates a set of enduring attitudes among the symptom-free as well as in those suffering from stress disorders. Among these attitudes are anger, alienation and guilt. These are not clinical symptoms at all but rather a new social, political, moral and religious consciousness brought about by events that overpower the psyche. This shift in consciousness is an appropriate response to a monstrously evil situation.

This new set of attitudes is not amenable to psychiatric treatment, because it is not a psychiatric problem. It is a cluster of fundamental questions about meaning, faith and the purpose of life. In cases of severe PTSD these questions are now seen as symptoms that are "refractory" (resistant to treatment), and they impede treatment progress unless they are confronted on their own terms. This means that even in psychiatric treatment, a successful outcome depends in some measure upon how well these larger questions are resolved.[2]

Janet believes that Xers who have experienced this changed awareness and have acquired these new attitudes often seem happier and more at peace than those who have not. There is a reason for this. What was previously a dim sense that something is wrong, a vague unease at the boundaries of consciousness, comes into focus. At last the problem can be "named." It is like when an alcoholic who has been denying the fact that the booze is in control finally comes to the realization that alcohol rules.

We find another analogue for the importance of altered consciousness in the Vietnam War. After the first exposure to combat, a soldier was no longer a "newbie" but understood experientially—and for the rest of his life—the full horror of it all. Veterans may have grieved for their lost innocence, but I never met anyone who wanted innocence restored. There is a certain satisfaction that comes with deeper understanding of life. This new awareness is also a fork in the road of life. One path can lead to nihilism, but the other road, as we shall see, leads to greater hope and peace than the innocent can ever possess.

In the case of Vietnam vets, a large segment of a total population suffered from clinical stress disorders—but not all or even most of the veterans. The war created questions of meaning, however, for *all* veterans and for most young adults of the Vietnam generation.

Generation X, the next generation after the Vietnam era, suffers from a double affliction: a great many of them have been traumatized in ways that cause PTSD (abuse, violence and so forth); but, more significantly, most of them are stressed out simply by living under current social conditions. The present social disorder is so great that simply being young today is a stressor for a huge segment of the twentysomething generation. I can find no other explanation for the widespread problems with stability, self-image, feelings of emptiness, depression, suicidal thinking, fear of the future and lack of hope among the young.

No single diagnosis encompasses these wide-ranging symptoms as did posttraumatic stress for Vietnam veterans. PTSD is now widespread among the young, but there are other clinical disorders that also seem to be prevalent among young adults. We will discuss some of these later.

Noted psychiatric researcher Richard Chessick, back in 1977, point-ed to some factors in Western society that could "spawn or facilitate" the development of one of these disorders, borderline personality disorder:[3] "Today's children are caught up in the current whirlwind of barbarism. This provides a counterforce from which only the very strongest adolescents can emerge unscathed."[4]

Chessick's enumeration of the features of our current "barbarism" is extensive and coincides with commonsense assessments made by many thinking people. The list includes the breakup of family, per-vasive instability of family life and loss of family as the ideal, loss of extended family, loss of moral values and religious traditions, a back-ground of affluence with no experience of hard times, inconsistency and insecurity of parents, high mobility and fast transportation, bom-bardment by television with its primitive sensations, and the general decline of social values and the quality of life in general.[5]

Abandonment and Alienation

Abandonment is a fundamental component of these disorders. The entire range of clinical symptoms and the consciousness that under-girds them stem from an abiding and painful sense of abandonment. The young have been abandoned by parents, loved ones, teachers, political leaders, even the culture itself. No one is really "there" for them now. This is nothing new for Generation X, because countless parents and other significant adults were not there for them in their childhood or adolescent years. More than any of their predecessors, they have been since birth a generation alone.

We see epidemic abandonment of the young most clearly in the lack of moral guidance and absence of concern for their spiritual well-being. In the United States this generation came of age at a time when we have degraded our national goals—life, liberty and the pursuit of happiness—into a venal grasping for personal satisfaction and instant gratification. This narcissistic embrace of the self is pervasive, infect-ing all our institutions and polluting our personal lives.

Twentysomethings do not remember another time. Their nearest elders are the "Baby Boomers"—that large population bulge, now in early middle age, whose sheer size has allowed it to dictate national trends. The Boom is arguably the most overtly self-centered generation in American history—older generations were better at masking their self-centeredness. Boomers, whose impact upon the culture is immense, always insisted on "doing their own thing" during their youth. Too many of them, it seems, continued to do so at their children's expense. No wonder resentment toward Boomers runs high among today's young adults. The Xers are a generation, as Janet points out, not wanted by their elders and not really liked.

Generation X is the most aborted of America's generations. It suffered the highest parental divorce rate—twice the rate faced by Boomers. Half of all marriages now end in divorce. One in four children is born to a single mother. As they grew to maturity, the second leading cause of death among Xers (after auto accidents) became homicide, followed by suicide.[6]

Generation X was born during the turmoil of Vietnam. Their introduction to politics took place in the Watergate-Irangate era of overt lies and deceit. The second generation raised on television, they have known the mass media only in their more manipulative and trivialized phase. Their exposure to educational systems took place at a time of national decline in schools' ability to teach effectively.

Tragically, this is not a local generational phenomenon. It seems to be true in other countries as well. My Russian friends tell me that even apart from the massive upheaval in the political and economic system in that country, there is a profound alienation among young people.

In a telephone conversation with one of the brothers from the religious community in Taizé, France—a place where thousands of young people from all over the world gather each week to pray, sing and reflect—the same word, *alienation,* came up. The brother told me that in his experience, young adults from all over the world seem to be increasingly alienated from their cultures.

Alienation is a state of deprivation, a lack of the most fundamental and necessary social connections. The alienated may seem fully engaged with others, but one detects a flatness of spirit in their relationships. Young people who have been abandoned and left to themselves are understandably wary and tentative, trusting little and withholding commitment. To be an alien means to be a stranger in a foreign land. The alien will not, cannot and perhaps should not trust the inhabitants of another country. The tragedy of alienated youth is that they are stangers in their *own* land, made so by their elders who denied them the deep and abiding affection that is the birthright of all children.

My own conversations and research confirm what Janet has found. One young woman, a college senior, related a conversation in which she and five friends were discussing their lives. She was the only one in the group whose parents were still married. She wondered "when that shoe is going to drop," meaning she had an irrational fear that her own parents—who are happily married—would divorce. She had been sexually abused (by a baby sitter and by a relative), so she could "chalk that one up." One other young woman was the only one in the group who had not been sexually abused; she wondered when it would happen to her. Conversations like this are commonplace.

As a parent of teenagers, I know that for those now in junior high and high school in America's cities, the fear of gang violence and drive-by shootings adds to stress even for those young people whose families are healthy. Fistfights have been replaced by gang fights with lethal weapons. The younger members of Generation X are even more deprived than their older sisters and brothers.

Those with no personal experience of such traumatic events are nevertheless aware that this is the way life really is for their contemporaries—and thus for themselves. They live with the very realistic expectation that something bad will probably happen to them. They know that life is hostile and dangerous. They have been abandoned.

They are alienated. They are alone.

Aloneness

So we have chosen Janet's term *aloneness* as the term that best describes the emotional, attitudinal and spiritual space Generation X now occupies. Aloneness is the enduring result of abandonment. It is the spiritual residence of those who have been abandoned. Aloneness goes beyond even the deprivation of citizenship in a community that is implied by the word *alienation.* In aloneness, one's life is filled with nothing but the clutter and busyness of activity and, all too often, the painful memories of one's own past.

There are nonclinical "symptoms" of life in our postmodern, pathological world. These are the basic questions of meaning that Generation X must resolve. They center on issues of abandonment, alienation and aloneness. A society in which we are free to abandon one another at our whim has no moral basis and cannot endure. No society that alienates its youth and sets them adrift can continue to exist, for it is already in a state of collapse. Either another, more moral and more viable social order will take its place or chaos will ensue. It is the business of Generation X to find a new vision and to bring about fundamental changes.

Giving birth to a new social order requires that we rediscover one another as persons and that we learn again how to love one another. Our primary spiritual quest is to find the God who continues to pursue us even in the depths of our aloneness.

Aloneness, that desolate place now inhabited by Generation X, can be a crossroad at which one may recognize that all the spaces within the soul have been trashed with the clutter of meaningless objects and debris from the past. One may acquiesce in this condition and continue sliding into the heart of darkness, where one can say of life only: "It don't mean nothin'." Or one may follow the restless currents within the spirit that lead again out of self-centeredness, toward others— and to God. This is the route from aloneness to genuine solitude, where the soul is filled with a holy emptiness.

Aloneness as solitude is the condition from which we are most able to join with another young adult many generations ago who found herself alone except for God. Her song comes down to us even today: "My soul magnifies the Lord, and my spirit rejoices in God my Savior, for he has looked with favor on the lowliness of his servant" (Luke 1:46-48).

2

GENERATION X: ITS PLACE IN HISTORY, ITS DESTINY

The City Built on a Hill (Bill)

Are the Boomers a yuppie generation? Janet and I look at it from two angles—one of us precedes the Boomers, one follows them. And to both of us Boomers look like a yuppie generation. But they're not the first. Yuppie seeds were planted in American soil as long ago as 1630, when John Winthrop declared that the colonists had a divine mission to build on the newly discovered continent a "city upon a hill." There would be hard work and sacrifice, but God would pour out upon the colonists the blessings of prosperity.

Those first residents of Massachusetts Bay Colony shared their governor's vision. They were willing to work hard, but they expected to be rewarded with a divinely guaranteed good life. Religious refugees from a tired old Europe, they were doing God's work, creating a "New Jerusalem" on the edge of an uncharted wilderness, and they were sure that God would bless them with earthly riches.

Thus were born both the American "work ethic" and the notion that "prosperity is our divine right." These impulses have endured for more than 350 years. Though our country has long since lost its original conviction that we are God's chosen people—that belief was simply a misguided version of the Old Testament kingdom of Israel— we continue to believe that we are uniquely favored among the earth's people.

Yet America's religious undergirding was deeply flawed from the start. Though committed Christians, our earliest American ancestors read the gospel through a warped lens. Jesus never promised his disciples material prosperity. On the contrary, he called us to walk the way of the cross with him. But despite this early distortion, the original "city on a hill" theology of our Puritan ancestors had a strong positive aspect: it connected public life directly to God and called upon individuals to work for the common good.

We have replaced this theology with a destructive and pervasive individualism in which the self is hermetically sealed off from others and seeks only "what's in it for me." We have adopted a secular religion of prosperity and have become a consumer society in which everything—our own humanity included—is a commodity.

No one could accuse the current yuppies of any kind of religious vision, but they are the legitimate spiritual offspring of America's first generation. Herein lies the problem for Generation X, the first Americans whose formative experiences have taken place during the collapse of the city on a hill. Generation X was raised amid the rubble of the New Jerusalem. Older Americans are discovering the ruins at midlife or in elderhood, but the city has already caved in upon the young.

Change Is the Only Constant

Some might argue that things are really much the same as they have always been. In this view nothing fundamental to the human condition changes very much. Generational divides, after all, are recorded as far back as twenty-five hundred years ago, with elders deploring the sorry state of youth, and the young for their part complaining about the world they inherited.

Intergenerational squabbles are sometimes funny. Some years ago, a newspaper interviewed a man who at the time was the oldest living American—he finally died at about the age of 130. He offered the stereotypical complaint that young people weren't much good these days—and then deadpanned, "I've been saying that for the past hundred years."

However much things remain the same, though, they also change. This has always been true, but it is truer than ever in our rapidly accelerating technological culture. It could even be said that change is now the only constant. Yes, "things have always been this way" in terms of the very basics of life, but it is equally true to say that things have always changed. The difference is that in times past events moved much more slowly—but historical change is always irreversible.

A few examples. The human race began supporting itself by foraging for food wherever it could be found. The transition from hunting and gathering to farming was permanent. Tools and weapons made of stone were supplanted by those fashioned from metal. The industrial age in turn replaced the simpler agricultural life through the mass production of goods. Again, humanity moved forward. We are now entering upon a "postindustrial" or "information age." No one doubts that this latest shift in the human condition will be permanent, yielding only at some future time to another era whose features we cannot now imagine.

Though historical periods have no clearly definable boundaries, Generation X is the first wave of humanity to reach adulthood on the "postindustrial" side of the new historical divide. Thus it sees the future more clearly than its elders. It is, in fact, formed as much by the world that is coming into being as by the world that has been. The social and emotional pathology so widespread among this generation of young people must be taken very seriously precisely because it represents one possible scenario for all of humanity's future.

The irreversibility of historical change refutes popular theories of generational cycles. According to one current interpretation, propounded by William Strauss and Neil Howe, generational changes are cyclic and fairly predictable, clustering around major inner awakenings and great events.[1] In this rendition, the first and dominant generation at the head of each cycle is a very idealistic one like the Boomers. It is followed immediately by a recessive, less favored, more practical, "reactive" generation such as Generation X.

Generation X in this reading would be the fifth American generation of "reactives" to follow dominant Boomerlike "idealists." The first idealists were—you guessed it—the New England founding Puritans. Their children, the first "reactives," much like present-day Xers, were roundly criticized by their moralistic, self-righteous elders.

According to Strauss and Howe, this cycle has been repeated four times previously in American history. Reactives and idealists have never liked each other very much—Xers and Boomers certainly don't—but they eventually make peace and decide to cooperate in raising children better. The result is another dominant generation called "civics," who are able to shoulder the burden of the next great national crisis and then assume leadership for a long period of time. The fading World War II generation is the most recent of these "civics." Sandwiched between the civics and the next idealists is a generation of "adaptives," who, like reactives, are a recessive generation caught between two dominants. The present "Silent Generation" (people in their fifties and sixties) are the current crop of adaptives.

Strauss and Howe bestowed the names upon these generations. They refer to Generation X as "Generation 13," because they are the thirteenth American generation since the United States began in 1776. We prefer "Generation X" because x in an algebraic equation has limitless possibilities—as does this generation.

A generation typically numbers among its parents members of the preceding two generations. Thus Xers had as their parents both Silents and Boomers. Children in the "Millennial Generation" (those born since 1982 and up through 2003) have or will have as their parents both Boomers and Xers. Strauss and Howe predict that these youngest Americans will become a "civic generation," better off than their immediate Xer predecessors, strong and dominant like the Boomers, and equal to the burdens of the next great crisis. In this theory, Millennials will benefit both from Xers' desire to give better parenting than they received and from the Boomers' supposed, if belated, conversion from narcissists into concerned midlife parents.

There is some validity to this rather clever interpretation of generational relationships, at least with respect to past history. But we believe there are several reasons that it is flawed as an indicator of the future. First, previous generational cycles provide no precedent for the rapidly accelerating pace of a global, multicultural, interdependent technological civilization. Never before has the linear direction and the unrepeatability of history been clearer.

The second reason for disputing this theory is that we see no evidence that Boomers—or any preceding generation—have undergone a conversion from narcissism, immorality, self-interest and greed. God, of course, continues to grant to individuals the grace of conversion from sin, but American culture is now clearly pervaded by a "what's in it for me?" mindset. People of all generations seem to be absorbed almost exclusively in themselves. We see no signs of a cultural change of direction.

The third reason for rejecting the prediction of a better life for Millennials and the continuance of the usual cycles for future generations is that the social and moral pathology inflicted upon Generation X is progressive. It is greater in the younger cohorts. The notion that somehow those born after 1982 will be less debilitated morally and socially than their immediate predecessors is pure fantasy.

Xers certainly have a clearer vision than do their elders of how harsh life is (this is characteristic of all reactive generations, according to Strauss and Howe). They undoubtedly have a greater desire than did the narcissistic Boomers in their young adulthood to spend their energies raising children well. But will Xers be able to accomplish this, or has society become so morally and spiritually bankrupt, as well as politically and economically exhausted, that the future holds only further decline?

Several possibilities lie in the future for the postindustrial age. These range from a much better world to a new dark age with a high-tech lifestyle and jungle morality. Generation X, always realistic, is not naive enough to rule out the latter scenario.

This clarity of vision with respect to life's true options is the reason one finds among Xers two apparently contradictory responses: some fall prey to hopelessness, while others are driven to work for change. Their religious attitudes go in two opposite directions as well. Countless young adults view the world as such a broken place that God must be irrelevant to real life. Others, however, especially the committed Christian Xers, having grasped so well the emptiness of contemporary life, turn to God from the deepest regions of their souls.

Modern and Postmodern

In order to fine-tune the vision of Generation X, we must consider the notion of the "postmodern" world. This is the era we are now entering as our "modern" world passes from the historical scene. In the postmodern world people can—and will—be replaced by technology. Let's look briefly at the development of these changes.

All ages, the modern era included, are shaped by great ideas. Political and economic systems, religious beliefs, philosophies, cultural assumptions and knowledge of the natural world are always interrelated, and within a culture they coalesce to form some sort of cohesive worldview. The modern era—which is now ending—really began in the seventeenth century, deriving its fundamental assumptions from two towering geniuses: Isaac Newton and René Descartes. Newton's physics made possible subsequent scientific progress, and Descartes provided the intellectual underpinnings for modern life.

The basic premise at the beginning of the modern era was the conviction that science alone could provide the answers to better living. It was thought that the human race was beginning an endless upward spiral in quality of life—all made possible by science. Religion and philosophy might remain, but they were no longer as important as they had been. In fact, religion was thought to be incapable of providing the basis for life. Evil would be eliminated in stages through greater knowledge and by the application of science to human problems.

We know now that things didn't turn out that way. The postmodern world is emerging now because the basic premise of modern life is flawed.

At this point I need to clarify that Janet and I are not reactionaries pining for a previous golden age—something that never existed. Nor do we demean or diminish the importance of the modern world's achievements. The last three centuries have been a period of immense progress. Democratic political systems, a global economy, effective medical treatment, scientific discoveries, technology—all have made the world a much better place than it was in times past. But this progress has had a downside. Being sinful creatures, we have continued to live out the story of Adam and Eve in the Garden—in the vastly destructive ways made possible by modern civilization.

At the dawn of modernity Newton showed that motion in the universe can be measured and is predictable. Newton quite rightly refused to use God as an explanation for any natural phenomenon. But scientific knowledge then became the norm for all knowledge. Since God was not to be found within the workings of nature, the knowledge of God was considered of little significance. Religious faith thus became irrelevant to real life. The "clockwork" universe was born, in which every particle influenced every other particle in predictable ways. God was, at most, the original artisan who fashioned the clock but subsequently remained uninvolved with its inner workings.

Descartes's seventeenth-century proclamation "I think therefore I am" coincided with Newton's laws of physical motion. It provided the clear and distinct ideas necessary to scientific progress. But it also inverted the relationship of our individual consciousness to everything that lies beyond the narrow borders of our thoughts and perceptions. What *I think* became the standard against which all reality is judged. Centuries of focus upon the *I* has led us from the "rugged individualism" of the American frontier to the pernicious individualism that now threatens to destroy our social fabric.

Psychology discovered the role of emotions—all to the good—but we have by now transposed Descartes into the key of emotions: "I feel, therefore I am." Therefore you, who are external to myself, exist to serve my emotional needs. Everyone and everything must contribute to my feeling good about myself.

Modern science led to the industrial age with its ability to mass-produce goods in great quantity and diversity—and with great benefit to humanity. But we are now able to believe in all seriousness, "I produce and consume, therefore I am"—the more I produce and consume, the more important I am. "I earn, therefore I am"—the more I earn, the greater I am.

The Transition Point

The modern world is ending because of several converging factors. In the realm of science, that all-important linchpin of modernity, concepts of reality have been so altered by twentieth-century physics that we can no longer accept the worldview that prevailed from Newton to the present. Einstein's relativity theories along with quantum mechanics and recent discoveries in astronomy have rendered all previously held positions obsolete. Reality is far more complex than we had imagined it to be.

Political, economic and social systems have grown correspondingly more complex. The intellectual undergirding of modernity has collapsed, and with it all the systems it spawned. Everywhere one looks it is the same. The world's economy is clearly undergoing a major and irreversible upheaval. No political system seems to work well. The democratic impulse may be growing around the world, but nationalisms, empires and even existing democracies seem to be unable to integrate the newly emerging yearnings for freedom. Communism has fortunately collapsed, but other political systems, our own included, are in serious trouble.

The "global village" has now become a reality through modern communications, but we do not yet know how to live in it very well. We confront each other more intimately as racially, culturally and religiously different, yet we are strangely distanced from each other because our meetings occur largely through electronic means of communication. We see each other on television, but we do not really interact.

A great spiritual hunger has arisen around the world as we repudiate the moral and intellectual emptiness of modern life and resist the impersonal forces of vast and dehumanizing systems. Yet we seem to find no answers to the crisis that accompanies the birth of the postmodern world. Everywhere we look we find decline.

Indicators of Decline: Economic

Today's young adults, having reached maturity in a time of great moral and spiritual bankruptcy, are also faced with economic ruin. They are the first Americans in history who cannot expect to achieve the economic success attained by their parents. About 20 percent of them now live in poverty. Already victims of the economic stagnation that has endured since 1973 and that forced both parents into the workplace during their youth, Xers as the most recent members of the work force have seen their median incomes fall faster than those of their elders. Fewer of them own their own homes—or can expect to own a home.

A generation ago, one full-time income was sufficient to support a family. Most American families now require the income of both husband and wife for survival, and there is growing evidence that even two full-time workers can no longer support a family at the middle-income level. Poor and lower-middle-class families are now falling behind even with both parents working. The multitude trapped in "McJobs" can't make it at all. Clearly, Xer parents will be more severely strained than were their own parents to find time to spend with their children.[2]

Economic turmoil affects all age groups, but the severity of impact seems to be inversely proportional to age. The older G.I. generation has done very well. They seem to have "won the generational lottery." Mostly retired and with pension benefits and social security well in place, they are insulated from the growing unemployment and underemployment that plagues younger workers. The American Association of Retired Persons (AARP) is one of the strongest lobbies in the nation. G.I.s are politically untouchable and are likely to remain the most favored generation in American history. The social security program faces bankruptcy in the future, but it will probably continue to provide benefits during the lifetime of the G.I. generation.

Silents, in their fifties and sixties, are currently at the top levels of management in business and most governmental agencies. Layoffs, job insecurity and limited retirement possibilities threaten some, but for the most part Silents remain insulated from hardship.

Boomers, the nemesis of Xers, seemingly ensconced in yuppie affluence, are beginning to lag behind their elders in net wealth. They started their working careers better off than their parents were at the same age, but they are now falling behind. They face a bleak economic future with the probable insolvency of the social security fund.

Young adults are hit harder than their elders by another phenomenon that seems to be overtaking America—we are showing the first signs of becoming a "Third World" nation. As in many impoverished parts of the developing world, we have seen a great widening of the income gap between rich and poor. We are increasingly becoming a nation of haves and have-nots. During the past twenty years, the gap between the percentage of income for those in the top fifth and those in the bottom fifth increased by 59 percent. The richest 20 percent of our population possess more wealth than do the remaining 80 percent. Within the top 20 percent, the highest 5 percent have more than the next 15 percent. At the very top of the economic pyramid, the wealthiest 1 percent are better off than the entire 4 percent immediately below them.[3]

The average pretax income of those in the top percentile grew by 77 percent in the twelve years preceding 1989. At the present time, half of all after-tax earnings go to the top 1 percent. During the same period, those at the median saw their incomes rise by 4 percent while the bottom 40 percent of families actually lost ground. These trends have been in place since the 1960s, and there is no indication of any change in the foreseeable future. All age groups are affected by the American slide into Third World status, but Xers begin their working lives assured that most of them will lose an uphill economic battle.[4]

These trends are not limited to the United States. The same forces are at work in all industrialized nations. It seems that the late stage of industrial or "modern" economies demands a "downsizing" that will impoverish most of the world's people. The situation is rendered more difficult by increasing confrontation between the expanding populations of the have-not nations and the industrial democracies. The world's poor—along with its refugees from war—are pouring across the borders of the more stable and developed nations. Intelligent young people around the world understand very well what these trends portend for them. The nihilism and loss of hope that characterize the global teen culture has a basis in fact. X is the most realistic of generations.

Yet there is nothing inexorable about these forces. Political and economic trends—even watershed historical shifts—are not absolute and predetermined like the laws of physics. Clarity of vision, awareness of what is taking place, is the first step on the road to change. Young adults need not lose hope. They must mobilize to radically change the world's political and economic institutions. Generation X, standing at the threshold of the postmodern era, has an opportunity given only to a few past generations—to imprint its stamp on a human epoch. Whether the world becomes a better place or enters a new dark age depends largely upon what Xers choose to do. Americans, citizens of the world's wealthiest and most powerful nation, will have an influence on the future disproportionate to their numbers. We have a marvelous opportunity—but we must seize it.

Moral Decay

Far worse than economic decline is society's moral and spiritual bankruptcy. In chapter one we discussed the impact upon Xers of simply being young in America today. The "new barbarism" inflicted on young people, which is the cause of their distress, is at root unbridled selfishness—the worst kind of immorality. It takes many forms, but most disastrous is family breakup. The diminishing of commitment that now characterizes American life is nowhere more evident than in the increasing willingness of marriage partners to call it quits. Sometimes divorce is necessary, but often it is mere convenience, allowing the partners to seek greater personal fulfillment elsewhere. The evidence is now in—divorce may benefit the spouses, but it causes severe trauma to children.

Barbara Whitehead writes, regarding our twenty-five-year national experiment in no-fault divorce:

The results of the experiment are coming in and they are clear. Adults have benefitted from the changes in family life in important ways, but the same cannot be said for children. Indeed, this is the first generation in the nation's history to do worse psychologically, socially, and economically than its parents. Most poignantly, in survey after survey the children of broken families confess deep longings for an intact family.[5]

Xers rate relationships ahead of every other need for a very good reason—vast numbers of them are victims of divorce. The relentless striving for human connectedness in Generation X is due in large part to early deprivation of the ongoing and consistent love of both parents. This is the reason Xers are determined to do better at marriage and parenting than did their elders.

Selfishness spawns many other offspring as well. Most of us realize through the experience of daily living that morality is rapidly disappearing from American life, and surveys confirm our commonsense perceptions. One of the most devastating American studies published recently reveals, among other things, that lying has become an integral part of our culture, we make up our own moral laws, we have lost faith in the institution of marriage, and we are the most violent industrialized nation on earth.[6]

The same publication reveals that our two top answers to the question of how we would change ourselves in order to better fulfill our potential are "I want to be rich" and "I want to be thin." Perhaps our national soul is not bankrupt; perhaps it is dead. Perhaps this is what Generation X understands.

These conditions are not limited to the United States; they seem to be global in scope. The United States merely leads the world's way into the future. The exhaustion of America's civil religion of individualism and prosperity coincides with the transition from modern to postmodern civilization. The United States had much to do with the creation of modern times and will doubtless influence for good or ill the shape of the era now beginning.

Xers, Prophets of Hope

The aloneness of Generation X is profound because it results from an intuition of the magnitude of our spiritual impoverishment. The meaning of life has collapsed around us, yet we proceed as if nothing had happened. Young adults know better. However much Boomers and other elders may protest, Xers perceive—dimly perhaps, but accurately—that hope has been eclipsed and love has vanished from the public culture.

Painful though it may be, Generation X must bear the burden of its intuition and the vision implicit within it, for this is a prophetic vision. As the founding generation of a new epoch, X must possess within its bones some sense of why the previous era collapsed; otherwise the future cannot differ from the failed past. Because no single age group acts independently of others, elders must begin to understand and appropriate the vision of Generation X. Humanly speaking, upon the excruciating difference between the intuitions of Generation X and those of its immediate predecessors rests the hope of the earth's future.

Again, history offers no guarantees. Today's young adults can opt to continue on the precipitous slope of moral and social decline rather than change course. But two qualities of Generation X lead us to believe that they will, in fact, choose a markedly different path.

The first is the element of suffering. Unlike Boomers, those supposed radicals of the recent past, Xers have acquired their perspective through societal and spiritual deprivation and are not likely to succumb naively to the blatant narcissism that was visited upon them.

The second quality is aloneness, which in its mature aspects bears striking resemblance to the religious and moral solitude of prophets, saints and mystics. Aloneness, as Janet points out, begins as a survival technique but seeks—and is redeemed when it finds—community. Authentic Christian spirituality always leads toward a common life, with others and with God. Xers, dissatisfied with the hollowness and clutter of life and often burdened by their own past hurts, seem to have an affinity with the virtue of humility. More than their elders, they seem generationally "poor in spirit." Poverty of spirit and humility are biblical qualities that are found among God's people in every era but that are at odds with the current spirit of the age. It seems that in Xers God is creating a predisposition to become authentically poor in spirit.

Going Beyond Constantine

The final opportunity open to Christians of Generation X—and to older followers of Jesus as well—is to participate actively, intelligently and with enthusiasm in refashioning the Church in ways that have not been possible for more than sixteen centuries.

American civil religion and modern civilization have existed for a little longer than three hundred years, but the Christian Church has based its relationship to all civil societies, premodern as well as modern, on assumptions that go back to the year A.D. 312.

In that year Constantine, who had been emperor of Rome for about six years, defeated Maxentius, his rival to the throne, in what history knows as the Battle of Milvian Bridge. Up until that time, Christians had been persecuted and despised by the Roman Empire. The worst persecution in Christian history had ended with the death of Emperor Diocletian in 305. After a few years of peace, however, Christians were still a threatened minority within the Empire. Before the battle with Maxentius's forces, Constantine had prayed to the Christian God and had emblazoned on the shields of his soldiers the first two Greek letters for Christ. After his victory, Constantine became a Christian and established Christianity as the official religion of the Roman Empire.

Subsequently, church and civil society became intertwined in ways that were sometimes beneficial and sometimes disastrous. The "Christendom" of the medieval and Renaissance periods did not really end with the Reformation, because both Protestants and Catholics carried with them fourth-century notions of how the Church relates to the world. American civil religion itself is a Constantinian distortion of the faith.

Modern secular culture presented a real threat to the Church and still tries to relegate faith to a role of insignificance. The Church in all its denominational forms and in all societies has rightly resisted the assaults of modernity, but unfortunately it has never freed itself sufficiently from its desire for a cozy Constantinian relationship to the culture.

As the modern world ends, with its spiritual emptiness exposed for all to see, two sides rush in to fill the vacuum—both with "power tools" left over from the Constantinian era. The first is a reborn "secular man," more determined than ever to eliminate from public life any reference to God. The second participant in the battle for the postmodern world is the fundamentalist: the Muslim, Jew, Hindu or Christian who is quite rightly unwilling to accept any further diminishing of transcendence, but who continues to rely on the power of the state or the surrounding culture for the enforcing of religious values.

The question has recently been asked: "Can we be good without God?"[7] Can a culture survive and flourish without some connection to God and without acknowledging values that transcend immediate goals? The answer, as the modern world has proved by default, seems to be no, we cannot live without God. But followers of Jesus cannot return to the "muscular" Constantinian Christianity that brought the Crusades, wars of religion, persecutions, inquisitions—and that is still so evident today in Northern Ireland, in what was once Yugoslavia, and also in the political battles that are being fought in the United States for the sake of religion.

Here again Generation X stands at a historical juncture. Young adult Christians intuitively demand more from the Church than what they have already experienced. The first postmodern generation can also be the first "post-Constantinian" Christians. We believe that young adult communities have already begun to emerge which will show to the world a different kind of gospel hope and love. This is nothing new, but rather a return to a very ancient way of Christian living.

Long before Constantine, the Church had already attracted thousands of converts because people could see "how these Christians love one another." A second-century emperor had even admitted publicly that the Christians cared more for the poor of Rome than he did. The power of our faith, then as now, lies in how we live the gospel of Jesus. The postmodern world requires a radical, profound Christian life and witness. We believe this is the vocation to which God is calling the Christians of Generation X.

Does this generation have within itself the power and resources to live this kind of life? Do any of us? The answer is, of course, that we do not. But the power is already given in the Lord. There is something quite peculiar about the way God works. The Spirit moves most freely in those who depend not on themselves but on God. Christian Xers, deprived of much that their elders took for granted, and with little esteem in the eyes of many, are well placed by God—precisely because they lack so much—to become the foundational generation of the post-Constantinian Church.

3
THE GOD SPACE

The Lightness of Being (Janet)

As we grow, spaces form within us. One of the earliest is the spouse space. When we are adolescents the space is vague and shifting in shape. But as we grow and discover who we are and what we want, the boundaries of that space become more defined. Soon we begin searching for one who will fit into our space. We go through life trying one after another to see if they will fit. Some fit for a while but change; some don't fit at all, but we try to squeeze them in. Some have no desire to ever enter into that space of ours. As that space becomes clearer and more defined, we become acutely aware of the emptiness inside. When finally, hopefully, we find one who fits, there is a simple slipping in, the door is closed, and we feel whole.

Eventually children spaces open up—more for some, less for others. As these spaces become more defined, the emptiness can become a painful longing. To fill children spaces, or spouse spaces, or friendship spaces takes much time, energy and thought. When these spaces exist, they need to be filled if we are ever to feel fulfilled and complete.

There is also a God space. In every human being there is a space inside for spirituality. This shape is the same for every person and is present in a very clear form from birth. It is larger than our other spaces—so large that many people cannot define it or see it is there. People for ages have attempted to fill this gaping emptiness with careers, alcohol, other people, drugs, activities or hobbies. Trying to fill the God space with such things is like tossing goldfish into the mouth of a whale. Only God can fill the God space. When we invite God into our space, we find the meaning of life. Literally. And a person cannot be truly fulfilled or truly complete until the God space is occupied.

The God space remains empty for many Boomers and Xers. I grew up in the God Is Dead era. It is no longer politically correct to mention God in public, and it is widely accepted now that a person's spiritual needs can be filled with material objects. How can we find meaning when the very Creator of meaning is not allowed to be mentioned? When and why did God fall out of pop culture?

Bill and I did some research among people of all ages by asking the following question: What is the most meaningful aspect of your life? People of older generations tended to answer "family" without hesitation. Among Generation X and those younger, answers ranged from "lunch" to "nothing." When they were pressed, though, their overwhelming response was "friends."

It seems it shouldn't need to be said, but it is difficult to find meaning in a world full of people you cannot trust. Consider what we find routine today. Carjackings; children bringing guns to school to protect themselves from other children; corruption in government; companies laying off tens of thousands of employees in order to increase their profit margin; unwed mothers; divorce. Because people have come to expect things like this, we suffer from a general lack of trust. How, when presented with this, does one find meaning in life?

Xers the world over are struggling because people today put so much meaning into their careers. During the times when Americans were working together to build their growing country or one of the many growing industries, it is understandable that they had tremendous pride in their work. But today's force of workers are continuously running into the wall of technology, which has taken much of the skill out of work and obliterated some careers altogether. The fact that we sought careers to find meaning and then found them to be meaningless has caused a great deal of anger and frustration. Some of us have simply dropped out, but some have left to find meaning in other places where we feel needed, where we can be doing something we consider meaningful.

Since the fall of the Iron Curtain, some twenty thousand college-educated American twentysomethings have moved to Prague to work as waiters, writers and English teachers. They are flocking to places where change is taking place rapidly and where their skills and energy can affect that change. There are many more examples of Xers heading in different directions in search of places where they might feel needed. It is their own search for meaning.

A woman named Tina got laid off from her job, so she moved to Berlin. Lisa said if she didn't get accepted to graduate school she would move to Corsica and be a bartender. Tony lost his job because his boss wanted someone older and more likely to stay around for ten years or more; his exemplary work was discredited by his generation's reputation. When he lost his job, he lost his will to compete in a world with those rules. Michael gave up a thirty-thousand-dollar-per-year engineering career because the long hours made it difficult to spend time with friends and family. He decided to live a much simpler life so he could enjoy time with people who are important to him. Andy and his wife sold their house and rented an apartment so they could spend more time and money on their children and less on home upkeep. These are typical Generation Xers.

The people of my generation have been finding meaning in life by seeking out situations in which they may have an affect in the world. Milan Kundera wrote a book titled *The Unbearable Lightness of Being.* This phrase made sense to me after I graduated from college, became settled in my career, found roommates and became completely independent for the first time. One day it occurred to me that any life decision I made, no matter how significant, would affect only me. If I wanted to move to Africa, quit my job, run for president, shave my head, go shopping after work, drop out, whatever, I could do so without altering the life of anyone else. It could be said that this is merely a phenomenon of growing up, but when an entire generation of people feel that no decision they make will affect anyone else, the sense of freedom can be suffocating. That is aloneness.

The past thirty years have taught us that we should do what we do for the effect it has on *us,* that nothing else matters. That philosophy has brought us the sexual revolution, drugs, junk bonds, skimming from savings and loans, and the use of tithes to pay for yachts. The "me generation" forgot about the unbearable lightness of being. This attitude has fostered things like gangs—people with little understanding of how their actions affect others. They have learned well the previous generation's lesson of narcissism.

What I and people of my generation want is simply for our actions and thoughts to mean something, to affect someone. This is why many of us wanted to stand with the students in China. This is why thousands of American Xers are living in Prague. This is why a thousand Xers rioted on a college campus for no apparent reason. Generation X is moving to, becoming part of or creating a world, a lifestyle or a community where our actions will affect those around us. We seem to be doing this instinctively.

The idea of a God who loves unconditionally, can be trusted and cares about our actions has been lost in recent years. My generation no longer believes in anything. The notion of God the Father has little meaning to the large numbers of people who grew up without a father. The miracle of the resurrection fails to impress a generation that simply does not believe in miracles, and the Church has become little respected as this generation sees many examples of corrupt leadership.

Yet there is a profound spiritual hunger within my generation. We are not convinced that "it don't mean nothin'." Xers are actively searching for meaning in the midst of this violent, changing, confusing time. Unfortunately, institutional religion offers little hope to us, for we no longer believe in or trust institutions. Besides, most Xers are hung up on the idea of sin. As Bill pointed out in chapter one, because of a widespread lack of self-esteem, references to sin are commonly taken very personally as a judgment upon oneself. One minister I know has taken to explaining sin as a breaking of relationships—one's relationship with God or with others.

How does this generation find God? How does it find the Church? And how does the Church find Generation X? Let's begin where we Xers have already begun. I believe we—members of this so-called apathetic, lazy, Peter Pan generation—are already going, perhaps at times unconsciously, in directions indicated by the gospel. We are, I believe, more "we-centered" than the "me-centered" Boomers. We value community, friendship, oneness and being part of something larger than ourselves. These are gospel values in secular dress.

Perhaps we are already halfway there in our search for God, for we are trying to fill the empty spaces within ourselves with relationships and friendship rather than material things. We are trying to reconstruct the family, and this is a process that resembles what Christianity offers. It is an apparently secular or earthbound search that is really oriented toward finding God. The Spirit is moving among my generation, teaching us new ways to fill the empty spaces in our hearts and subtly, unobtrusively, calling on us to recognize the true nature of that largest of all spaces within the soul.

The Earthbound Search (Bill)

Lunch in a university cafeteria is never an elegant affair, but the conversation often is. The student sitting across from me had just described succinctly his generation's spiritual inclination. "Our spirituality," he said without apology, "is earthbound." This is clearly one direction of the generational search for meaning I have found among Xers. Janet's research and her comments confirm this.

In a sense, X is a more earth-centered generation than any of its living predecessors. How could it be otherwise, given modernity's centuries-long drift away from transcendence? Not only are Xers the children of the Boom and Silent generations, but they—and we—are the spiritual offspring of modern Western culture.

We must look closely, however, at another feature prominent in the spiritual quest of the first truly postmodern generation. Xers are, as Janet reminds us—with their emphasis on community, friendship and oneness with others—trying to be part of something larger than themselves. We must discover what is implicit but unstated in this attempt.

A very simple and direct approach to finding community is what Janet told me about in one of our many conversations. She called it "the spirituality of dinner together." While in college, she was able to find among her peers people who were "exhausted" by the lack of trust in their world. They wanted to be a part of a community of people they could trust. They created this community by cooking dinner together.

Janet characterizes the spirituality of her generation as "we-centered" and contrasts it with what she believes to be the "me-centered" spirituality of Boomers. I am convinced that the difference she describes is real but represents more than merely a generational contrast between X and Boom. It is potentially a shift of tectonic proportions in the religious culture.

An outside observer of Generation X soon encounters an aspect of its spiritual search that seems to negate the quest itself. Many Xers simply find no meaning in life and do not expect to find any. Why not go on a whim to "tend bar in Corsica"? After all, that makes as much sense as anything else. I find similar responses frequently in my conversations with young adults. Not long ago I asked a young woman who is an active member of her parish church what gave her life most meaning. Her reply: "Nothing." Such an answer can denote, as we shall see, the first step into nihilism, or it can mark the beginning of a march into the deeper regions of faith.

A final feature of the search for meaning within Generation X bears close examination. Janet believes that Xers are "halfway there" in the explicit search for God because their secular values are closer to the gospel than are the prevailing values of American culture. As Janet once told me about her generation, "All we have is humility." At first glance the assertion seems not only generationally self-serving but also contradictory to X's earth-centeredness and incipient nihilism. It is neither, as we shall see, but rather a recognition that some human values are indeed closer to the gospel than others.

Finding Meaning in Spineless Reality

Janet and I have emphasized in previous chapters the social, economic, moral and religious decline that confronts young adults, youth and children in our culture. This decline amounts to real hostility toward the young. Malevolence of this kind causes those it affects to question the goodness of life, their own self-worth and even whether existence is worthwhile.

We all have a primal intuition into the nature of reality. We know innately, instinctively, without recourse to reasoning or deduction, "the way things really are." This primal intuition is the foundation for our attitudes and beliefs about everything. It is acquired simply by living. Though it can be altered throughout life, the experiences of childhood and youth are decisive in its formation.

I remember that my generation and the Boomers who followed us assumed without question that reality was benevolent, nurturing and structured. As children and young adults we all accepted the social system without much question; in the days before we became aware of the ecological crisis, we also had no questions about the stability and endurance of our natural environment. Our primal intuition about reality was that it is fundamentally good.

The famed Boomer rebellion of the sixties took place with the understanding that society was stable and secure enough not only to tolerate dissent but even to change because of it. Boomers were well-protected and even pampered rebels. For Boomers and for all of us elders, reality was "vertebrate." It had spine and was predictable.

Xers, on the other hand, assume that social reality is like a malevolent jellyfish. It has no spine, no structure, no predictability, no safety. Nothing is certain, nothing can be trusted. Even the individual's relationship to nature in a world of ecological deterioration is problematic—humanity's ancient assumption that nature is a constant has disappeared along with other certainties. Reality for Xers is in economic, political, ecological, moral, religious and cultural free fall. It is completely up for grabs. It is, like the jellyfish, "invertebrate."[1]

The contrast between structured and jellyfish constructions of meaning are so great that not only are the answers dissimilar, but even the questions are different. Thus there is a profound and crucial difference between the primal intuition of Xers and that of their elders. When all is free flow, it makes equal sense to tend bar in Corsica, to make a million dollars, to drop out—or do anything else. Finding meaning in lunch and having no purpose at all are equally viable within a jellyfish world.

Society exists, after all, to establish a common life for its citizens. It is supposed to afford us genuine access to one another so that we may mutually fill those vacant spaces within us, all the while leaving open the aperture to the God space. For Xers, society does not deliver these goods.

When a culture has declined so far as to attempt to fill all the spaces in the heart with what has been called "the Imperial Self," that civilization is intellectually and morally dead.[2] The first step in creating a new world is the refusal to assign meaning to the old one. By pointing out to us that the reigning cultural emperor has no clothes,

Generation X has begun the intellectual subversion of an era that must necessarily pass from the scene. Boomers trimmed some branches from the cultural tree, but Xers are attempting to lay the ax to its root.

To use a biblical metaphor, it seems that at least some members of Generation X would like to tie a "millstone about the neck" of modern civilization and drown it "in the depth of the sea."

Culture as Stumbling Block

Jesus, holding in his arms a young child, had some very harsh things to say about anyone who placed a "stumbling block before one of these little ones who believe in me." Better for the person who did so, he continued, "if a great millstone were fastened about your neck and you were drowned in the depth of the sea" (Matthew 18:6; also Mark 9:42). Jesus' language here is very strong. The Greek word for "stumbling block" is *skandalon,* from which we derive our English *scandal.* Some translations (such as the NIV) treat the word as meaning "offense" or "things that cause people to sin."

Jesus then lamented: "Woe to the world because of stumbling blocks!" (Matthew 18:7).

The words of Jesus are clearly directed against those individuals who "scandalize" or lead others, especially young people, into sin. But there is a sense in which the cumulative effect over time of countless individual amoral choices and actions so corrupt a culture that it becomes itself a stumbling block to its youth.

Great numbers of Xers are former Christians. These are people who attended church and Sunday school as children and in early adolescence, but for whom religious faith is no longer important. This is a different phenomenon from "taking a vacation from church," common among young adults of previous generations—though some Xers are doing this as well.

I believe we find among Generation X a vast multitude who are genuinely "post-Christian" people. Religious terms like *God, Jesus, church* are of no greater significance for them than, say, *money, job, career.* There may be many reasons for this, but primary among them is the tragic fact that we Christians ourselves are in such hot pursuit of the "Imperial Self" that we have become indistinguishable from the surrounding culture. Though numerically dominant in the American version of modernity, we have allowed its moral and religious spine to disintegrate. We ourselves have become the jellyfish our young so rightly repudiate. By doing so we have become an offense or scandal to our young, especially those of whom Jesus spoke "who believe in me."

My first inkling that a culture with large numbers of Christians could become an offense to others came during my first years in the ordained ministry, while I was serving as a missionary in Japan. Japan, thirty years ago and now, has a Christian population that is only about 1 percent of the total. I was attempting to explain how it is that Jesus can change our lives to a college student who, though a nonbeliever, had some sketchy knowledge of the Bible. He asked me whether most American servicemen were Christians. I stated rather proudly that they were. Then he asked, "Why then do almost all the Christian servicemen use the whorehouses around military bases?"

Seeing that I had no good answer to that one, he led the discussion toward issues of war and peace. "How," he asked, "do you explain the firebombing in 1945 of Tokyo and Nagoya and the atomic bombing of Hiroshima and Nagasaki?"

Knowing I had him, I responded, "And how do *you* explain Pearl Harbor?"

Smiling, he replied, "But we Japanese do not pretend to be Christians."

In that conversation I encountered for the first time the obstacles to belief posed by the failure of Christians to be true leaven transforming society. Though there are many other reasons that the faith has not taken root in Japan, a major barrier is the behavior of Christians. As the Christian elements of Western civilization continue to erode even though a huge segment of our population considers itself Christian, increasing numbers of our own young are asking, "Why *should* we believe?"

Avenues to Belief in a Post-Christian World

Unlike Japan, which has no historical Christian roots, European-American civilization still bears some resemblance, however defaced, to the faith that transformed it many centuries ago. Japan's Christian community, a tiny minority, bears far less responsibility for the moral and religious directions of society than does the Church in the West. My Japanese student friend was "scandalized" by the behavior of people of a religion that is extraneous to his cultural experience. American Xers are "scandalized from within," for the faith that no longer provides meaning to them is one they know from the experience of growing up.

Christianity is for X, as it was for preceding American generations, an integral part of growing up, but its impact on elders and Xers is fundamentally different. For all elders, including Boomers, the Christian faith was a formative influence—in fact, the transforming element—at the heart of a nurturing society. For Xers the same faith is the moral and religious center of the very society that gave birth to them and then cut them adrift. The Christian transformative influence has gone in the wrong direction for Xers. As they quite properly look in new places for fundamental meaning, many of them simply cannot consider Christianity as a serious option. They are in this very basic sense "post-Christian."

How then can Xers rediscover meaning in the ancient faith that is God's gift to all generations? We believe that the search for meaning and for God consists in finding amidst the entities that fill the various spaces within the Xer soul the "unknown God" whose traces are so clearly there.

The Unknown God

The New Testament contains the model for the Church's mission to

Generation X. It is found in the seventeenth chapter of Acts. Paul had arrived in Athens, which, though it was no longer the political and military capital of the ancient world, was still its cultural and intellectual center. Invited to explain his teaching to the council of the Areopagus, a group of intellectuals, Paul tried a new approach. He noticed that among the statues dedicated to the various gods worshiped at the time was one erected "to an unknown god." With profound insight, Paul realized that the Athenians really worshiped the true God amidst the idols of religious confusion. But they were ignorant of who this God really was. Paul decided to make explicit the worship that was already implicit among them.

In a brilliant missionary statement, Paul first acknowledged that the Athenians were "extremely religious . . . in every way" (Acts 17:22). Drawing on their innate religious impulse, which was demonstrated by the presence of this statue, Paul then proclaimed to them the truth about who it was they worshiped as the unknown god.

His proclamation of Christ to the Athenians resulted in only a few converts, so history has dismissed his effort as largely unsuccessful. This is not the case, however, for Paul had planted a seed that his successors nurtured to full growth. The subsequent conversion of ancient Greek and Roman civilization to Christianity was as complete as any conversion has ever been.

We now find ourselves walking for the first time into the emerging edifice of a postmodern, post-Christian and post-Constantinian Areopagus. Generation X, inhabitants since birth of this new Areopagus, are, like their ancient Athenian counterparts, "extremely religious . . . in every way."

Christian Xers like Janet have already begun to identify the ways in which their peers are very religious. The apparently secular, life-affirming, we-centered, earthbound spirituality we have already discussed is the specific way in which Generation X is very religious. The essential first step in the Christian mission to Generation X is to appreciate their spirituality for the divine gift it is. It is the way in which they are grasped by the God who is at this time unknown to them. The second step is to live and proclaim the gospel among them so as to render explicit and identifiable the living God who calls them in Jesus Christ. This must be done in two ways, I believe.

First, Xers—and we elders—must ourselves plunge into the very core and heart of our faith, leaving aside the centuries' accretions, the baggage that obscures some fundamental elements of basic Christianity. For example, success-oriented, achievement-driven, God-wants-you-to-be-prosperous religion bears no resemblance to the message of Jesus. Neither does the spiteful harshness of fundamentalism or the squishy psychobabble of contemporary religious liberalism—the voices that now frame American religious discourse. These are all part of the trappings of, or reactions to, moribund modernity and are no longer adequate to convey the gospel. They are part of the scandalous stumbling block that has rendered the gospel inaccessible.

The second step along the path to discovering the One who alone can fill the God space is for Xers to follow the inclinations of their hearts, which are leading them in ways Janet has described. Searching for friendship and community, attempting to become part of something larger than themselves and becoming we-centered, are indeed, as Janet asserts, life-affirming instincts. Confronted with a culture that is spiritually dead, Xers, with a primal intuition that is alive and functioning, have gone in a direction that is truly halfway to the gospel.

The gospel thus intersects with the spiritual trajectory of Generation X in the implicit, inarticulate knowledge of God to be found in Xers' struggles and yearnings. The widespread alienation of young adults from their Christian faith has resulted in a largely unfilled God space among Xers. Generation X does not yet have much of a "theistic compass" with which to navigate life. But the values Xers hold dear are closer to the Christian emphasis on seeking and serving others than is the narcissistic thrust of the culture. We-centeredness is closer to the gospel than me-centeredness. A spirituality of cooking dinner together bears more resemblance to biblical community than does the relentless pursuit of money and power.

Generation X has going for it an affinity with the second of the two great commandments, the love of neighbor—which is at least a start on the road to the first and greatest commandment, the love of God. Its apparently secular drift is really the beginning of the kind of religious transformation necessary to combat the evils of our age. But only a Church renewed and transformed can show to post-Christian Xers the God whom they seek.

The Christian sermon on the steps of the postmodern Areopagus thus begins with removing the stumbling block to faith that we have placed. When we ourselves, Christian Xers and elders, become more we-centered and life-affirming, humble, nurturing of our young, less driven by materialism, Generation X may begin to see in us the living God who desires residence in the God space of everyone.

The Absent God

The spiritual journey of Generation X intersects with the gospel at another point. Xers and we elders who share in the wasteland of late modernity must explore again in our own time the ancient and profound paradox that lies at the heart of Christian faith: God is both present to us and absent from us. And those times when the divine absence is most painful are moments of great grace in which God is really closer to us than when we seem to be basking in spiritual sunlight. As we shall see in a later chapter, this is a truth of immense significance for each individual on the voyage to eternity, but it is also a fact that defines the spirituality of generations and epochs.

American Christianity from its beginnings until the present has been rooted in the experience of God's nearness to us—and our nearness to God. This is an authentic and biblical experience, but it represents only one part of the paradox. The other part, the felt absence of God, is equally authentic. The religious experience of Generation X is at odds with the "God is near" paradigm. As is so often the case with this generation, the shift really began long ago, with the secularism of the nineteenth century, and has continued unabated. But Xers grew into maturity as the culture enthusiastically and unashamedly embraced a world without God. Xers grew up on the secular side of the paradigm shift. That God is absent to so many of them should come as no surprise. The God revealed in Scripture is both intimately present to us and, at the same time, painfully absent.

Jesus on the cross experienced in a profound way the absence of God: "My God, my God, why have you forsaken me?" (Matthew 27:46) is nothing if not an experience of God's absence. But his final statement recorded in Luke's Gospel, "Father, into your hands I commend my spirit" (23:46), expresses an awareness of God's loving presence. Jesus, on the cross, in the very act of our redemption, experienced both God's presence and God's absence. The experience of Jesus remains decisive for Christians in every age.

All Scripture reveals the present-absent mode of God's being for us. The first book of the Bible tells us that God created the heavens and the earth and all that is in them, including humanity, and then saw that all creation was "very good" (Genesis 1:31). Creation can be "very good" only because it exists in God's hand—because it basks in God's presence. But Scripture also tells us that humanity, God's special creation, rebelled and suffered exile from God's familiar presence in the Garden (Genesis 3:23-24).

The entire New Testament is the story of God's intimate presence among us through the Word of God who took on our own flesh. And yet the New Testament ends with a prayer that acknowledges the Lord's absence: "Come, Lord Jesus!" (Revelation 22:20).

Paul, that most subtle of all biblical writers, argued on the one hand that God's effective presence—the kind of presence that leads us to our eternal destiny—is found only in Christ Jesus. We perceive God's presence through a kind of experiential knowledge that is given to us by the Father through Christ in the Holy Spirit. Yet Paul also recognized that all humanity possesses an implicit knowledge of God (Romans 1:18-23). Paul merely repeated what every Jew already knew—

that only the fool says in his heart, "There is no God" (Psalm 14:1; 53:1).

Here again, the spiritual voyage of Generation X, seemingly at odds with traditional Christianity, is really very close to the heart of the gospel. Xers see the shallowness of a Church that cannot deal with the absence of God from our culture or with the real forces of darkness that surround us. They cannot relate to a Church that denies the reality that oppresses them. The only Church Xers will recognize is one that walks with Jesus the way of the cross and cries out with him in their behalf.

The Restless Heart

Even in the best of circumstances, when most of the spaces in the heart are filled—when one basks in the presence of a loving spouse, when children bring joy, when friends truly comfort and console, when work is pleasant, rewarding and well paid—there is an emptiness at the center of one's being. The God space remains a gaping hole at the center of existence, for it can be filled by God alone. Often this truth remains hidden for years as people pursue other options, discovering only over time who it is that fills this space. For Xers, denied fulfillment in their youth of so many human spaces, it is possible to come earlier in life to recognize the One who fills our emptiness.

Among the many features of Xer aloneness is its restlessness. Those who are alone and can trust no one desire more than anything else to be able to trust. Those who are not needed desire to be needed. Those whose lives are filled with meaningless clutter desire to find some meaning that corresponds with what their primal intuition tells them is true. Persons who see themselves as random molecules and for whom personal encounters consist in bumping into other molecules cry out for authentic humanity. Those who are alone are truly, authentically, spiritually restless—always on the move, searching for deliverance from their aloneness.

In this restlessness lies the real possibility of discovering another classic Christian truth, stated best by Augustine, the fourth-century North African bishop. He wrote in his autobiographical *Confessions* a sentence that applies preeminently to a generation restless and alone. It is one of the greatest sentences in all religious literature: "You have made us for yourself, O Lord, and our hearts are restless until they rest in you."

Augustine simply stated a fundamental Christian truth, one that applies to every age and every place. It is, I believe, a truth that is more accessible to Generation X than to most American Christians, whose restless hearts have been numbed and whose minds have become distracted by the toys technology has produced. Xers are notoriously cynical and suspicious of advertising, of politics, of promises that can't be kept. They tend to view society as hollow, meaningless and built on false promises. They know they are alone and searching for relationships. They admit they are restless.

The postmodern Church that will be the body of Christ for Generation X must be a restless Church, a Church constantly on the move, fostering relationships, caring for people, feeding the hungry—a Church not pining for political power or material benefits, but a Church always on the move toward its risen Lord.

A Church That Moves with God

As the Church moves toward the risen Christ who beckons to it and calls it into being, it must necessarily be "post-Constantinian." It must be the restless postmodern Church we have described. This Church cannot be peripheral to Generation X or to subsequent generations. It must be at the very heart and center of life, for it is the body of Christ. It can only take this position if it speaks to the real-life issues of young adults. As we have seen, this generation has arrived early in life at that crossroad—in previous generations reached much later—where one must choose between nihilism and despair on the one hand and ultimate hope and peace on the other.

The generational "altered consciousness" produced by youthful exposure to evil that we have already described has brought about this earlier arrival at the crossroad. The scandalous nature of our culture ensures that Xers will remain perched at this crossroad until something impels them to move in one direction or the other. Such an impulse will likely take the form of a gentle encounter between those with a more nihilistic bent and those who see hope. Realists always, some Xers have found that they can search together, not only for meaning but also for practical ways out of the various impasses in their lives. They seek meaning in a way that runs counter to the individualism of our society—they do it in community.

The Church is the community gathered by God, and so it must offer examples of real community. The leaven among Generation X are those young adults who are forming communities among themselves and with God. For indeed there is a path out of hopelessness and into transcendent hope. It lies in community, and ultimately in community with God. Along the way, the voyagers find healing of broken spirits, deeper relationships, ways to change the world and, finally, ways to encounter the God who is the giver of these gifts.

The rest of this book will describe how God is already moving among Xers, healing, imparting meaning and purpose, fostering relationships, gathering those who are alone, showing new ways to feed the hungry and give drink to the thirsty. We believe that God, whom Augustine described as "ever Ancient, ever New," is already at work with an Xer blueprint, reshaping, enlarging and renovating that space which lies deepest within the heart. And God is already moving in.

4

THE HEALING COMMUNITY

Telling the Truth Together (Janet)

The "Generation X salons" I held in my home began the weekend of the 1992 Los Angeles riots. We talked for hours about the hatred we saw and the fear and anger we felt. We talked about how we were afraid of being black or white or Mexican or Asian, because we were afraid we too could be attacked without provocation. We feared driving our cars because they might be "carjacked." We talked about how it no longer mattered where we lived, we always felt vulnerable to attack. We were angry at the betrayal of our fellow human beings; we felt chronic fear and a lack of trust in others.

The people whose homes were damaged, whose stores were looted by armed children or who were randomly beaten by vicious crowds will likely require the kind of therapy that has been developed to treat posttraumatic stress disorder. Like the Xers who met in my home, these people have reported deep feelings of betrayal, chronic fear and a complete loss of trust.

We shared symptoms with the victims of the riots, but our aloneness wouldn't be healed by therapy. We needed to be in a place where we could, if only for a few hours, prove that there was safety and there were people we could trust. It took therapy to heal the wounds of the riot victims, but it takes community to heal the wounds of aloneness.

The Prism of Distrust

The large number of today's youth who have suffered some form of abuse or neglect is matched by an equal number who have never suffered abuse yet see the world through the prism of that hurting half. Those who learned love, responsibility and nurture at home must interact daily with those who learned early to rely only on themselves and that to survive it had to be "me first." Those who survive by the "me first" motto necessarily see the world through a prism of distrust. Now, though, even those who were not raised that way find it necessary to see the world through a similar prism in order to protect themselves. For this reason, no one is exempt from feelings of aloneness.

Because of the prism many Xers look through, there are many who suffer symptoms similar to those of posttraumatic stress. Because of their view of the world, they feel hopeless, afraid or ambivalent about the future; they lack trust and close friendships and often feel torn between what they feel society expects of them and the way they want to be. Instead of asking "Who am I?" Generation X is asking, "Who am I going to be?"

A woman my age, Lydia, had grown up in a stable home. For some time she dated Craig, who was raised by an abusive father. Both his parents had worked outside the home. While he was growing up, he had been told over and over by his father that he was worthless and would never amount to anything. Craig spent his entire life trying to prove his father wrong; fiercely he pursued high-paying jobs, expensive cars and "important" friends. None of it worked, though, because his parents never acknowledged his achievements. As a child he had learned early on that he could rely only on himself and that the only way to get ahead was to think "me first."

Lydia found that she could never rely on Craig. He said he could never get married because marriage meant nothing to him, and much as he desired Lydia's love and friendship, he was never able to accept it because he didn't feel he deserved it. When Lydia asked him to put more into their relationship, he felt trapped and angrily pushed her out of his life.

Lydia, who had grown up knowing love, support and respect, was left with a residue of distrust and anger. She wondered if she would be ever able to trust anyone again. Both she and Craig were left feeling very alone.

The *Los Angeles Times Magazine* recently carried a story about a group of friends who were driving down a city street at night. At a stoplight they noticed that the car next to them did not have its lights on. But when they flashed the universal signal to let the driver know, he only stared at them. They shrugged, the light turned green, and they drove off. The lightless man followed them for blocks until the friends turned into a parking lot, whereupon the man began to shoot at them. The owner of the car, a young woman, was shot and died in the back seat. When the police caught the man, he said he had shot at them because he thought they were being disrespectful.

The trauma experienced by the girl's friends, as well as the abuse Craig suffered in childhood, can and should be treated with therapy. But how do you heal the anger and distrust that have been fostered by the fact that every other person we deal with is a Craig? How do you treat the thousands who read that story about a woman's being shot for her politeness? What do you tell people who have no more hope?

Two thousand years ago, the disciples saw Jesus—a beautiful, innocent man—arrested. He was a victim of preposterous accusations which everyone knew had been cooked up by a corrupt, scared government. Then they watched as this man—whom they'd seen healing the sick, feeding the needy, comforting the sorrowful and raising the dead—was stripped, spit upon, blindfolded, whipped, mocked, paraded through town and crucified. Everything they believed in was bleeding on a cross and dying. Where was hope there?

Just before his death, the robbers being crucified next to Jesus spoke, and one said, "Remember me when you enter your kingdom." And Jesus told him, "Today you will be with me in paradise."

Even in that desolation, when the disciples thought all was lost, Christ was King. There *was* hope. The disciples saw him raised from the dead—and they never again knew a loss of hope.

Generation X and the disciples just before Jesus' death have a lot in common. For them, hope seems only a word. People all over have experienced aloneness, some because of abuse and some because of the residue of hopelessness that has washed off onto them. We all need hope.

The Spirituality of Dinner Together

While in college, I began noticing small pockets of resistance, pockets of trust. People who had the courage to be vulnerable—but in a group. That was the key. It makes so much sense when I look at it now, that people who suffer the same grief would congregate and hold each other up, simply because they know the same pain. These groups were not Twelve-Step programs or counseling groups; not all of us had been abused or neglected children. But we did feel traumatized and rather exhausted by the lack of trust in the world. We wanted desperately to be part of some community of people we could trust. So we created this community by cooking dinner together.

We cooked together often, and found a spirituality in it that we couldn't find in church or in any therapy session. What we did was create a family, a community—something larger than ourselves, but not so large that our individual actions did not have an effect. We sought healing of our broken spirits in the community of others, and we found it.

Some of us need therapy; some do not. What Bill and I have found in creating communities for Xers is that regardless of the need for therapy, aloneness is healed only by being part of a community. And as Bill will explain and psychiatrists will attest to, no amount of therapy can fully bring healing until the God space is filled.

A Generation of Survivors (Bill)

Fear, distrust, burdens from the past: all exert a lifelong influence on the way a person functions and relates to others. Xers in large numbers continue to bear the wounds of childhood, early assaults upon the self. But healing of the self takes place in many ways.

Janet's perspectives and mine on healing the self are different. Hers is a view from within Generation X, and in this chapter she speaks from her personal experience of those affected by the serious trauma of others. As we shall see, this "indirect effect" exerts a significant influence on the entire generation. My own perspective, because I am a generational outsider, is more clinical and pastoral.

Janet's is a uniquely Xer dilemma. Though the childhood and youthful experiences she describes occur among young people everywhere and always, the problem specific to Generation X is that of "critical mass." This term comes from physics and refers to the amount of radioactive material necessary to initiate and sustain a chain reaction. The myriad familial and social pathologies we have described in previous chapters have, in Generation X, reached sufficient proportions to set off a chain reaction of pathology within the entire generation.

As Janet often reminds me, X is a generation of "survivors." When life is difficult, coping skills are developed and the resilience of the human spirit comes into play. Motivated perhaps by a desire to be different from their Boomer elders, Xers strike out in new directions.

Janet and I both know twentysomethings whose fortysomething parents are still living out their flower-child fantasies—trying to "find" themselves, doing drugs and attempting to recover the Woodstock

lifestyle. Though the Xer children of these families have been sub-
jected to parental neglect, and often abuse, their resilience carries the
day and they become more mature and wholesome adults than their
parents will ever be. Some of them have become the most effective
leaders of the "resistance movement" to recover community. The
dross of their early lives has become the gold of full maturity and
emotional health.

The Need for Therapy—Sometimes

Some Generation Xers need a community with a specific healing
focus. Among the most effective healing communities are the informal Twelve-Step meetings of Alcoholics Anonymous (AA) and its various offshoots like Narcotics Anonymous (NA), Alanon and Alateen.
The principles of AA are widely known and practiced. Xers, like many
in previous generations, have benefited from Twelve-Step healing.
Such a recovery program is simply a *must* for anyone with an addiction
problem.

The community of family or friends is where most healing takes
place. But there are times when the special expertise of a trained
psychotherapist is needed to complete the process. Most of psychotherapy consists in listening. But a therapist listens with a trained ear
and is prepared to guide a person through some hidden dangers in
the healing process.

Rape and sexual abuse, tragically, occur with great frequency
among Xers. These events always require therapeutic intervention. In
my own pastoral counseling, I refer the victim to a professional therapist, and I recommend involvement with a group of people who have
undergone similar experiences.

In places like the cities of Southern California—and now in other
cities across the land—another kind of assault upon the self is rapidly
becoming a fact of life for members of Generation X. People who have
been exposed to family or gang violence or who have witnessed or
survived drive-by shootings are almost always in need of counseling.

Dealing with Posttraumatic Stress

Such violent events "outside the range of usual human experience," if unresolved, lead to posttraumatic stress disorder (PTSD).[1] I have already discussed PTSD in a previous chapter, but several things remain to be said about it. Natural disasters such as earthquakes and plane crashes can bring about PTSD, but the "disorder is apparently more severe and longer lasting when the stressor is of human design," as it is in combat, rape, sexual abuse, and family and gang violence.[2]

The primary effect of PTSD is "emotional anesthesia" or "psychic numbing" by which the person attempts to escape the emotional impact of what has happened. The sufferer makes deliberate efforts to avoid thoughts or feelings about the traumatic event and attempts to avoid situations that resemble the event. This is always futile, because the event continues to intrude by way of dreams and sleep disorders, depression, anxieties, suicidal or homicidal thinking, rage, flashbacks and the like. In the case of rape or sexual abuse, PTSD can so inhibit a person that a normal healthy sexual relationship becomes impossible. Many people avoid marriage altogether or suffer sexual frustration in marriage because they have been raped or abused. The capacity for the emotional intimacy required for sexual companionship has been destroyed and must be restored. Some kind of therapy or group experience is crucial.

Family or gang violence, like combat, also intrudes upon a person throughout life. Any kind of violence destroys the capacity for emotional and even sexual intimacy, because one experiences fellow humans as hostile and destructive. This is the reason PTSD is more severe when caused by human actions rather than natural disaster.

In therapy, a skilled person provides an emotionally secure context in which painful experiences of the past may be remembered and resolved. Therapy is usually itself a painful experience at first, because the emotions connected with the traumatic event reemerge. This time, however, they are confronted in the open and allowed to run their course. Grief, guilt, anger and the other emotions surface at the conscious level and find resolution.

The therapist is a necessary guide to the discovery of real community. But therapy cannot be a permanent substitute for interpersonal relationships, family or the larger community with others. It is but a step along the way, necessary for some but not for all.

Borderline Personality Disorder and Identity Disorder

What I have said of PTSD is true also of the other clinical disorders that afflict Xers in large numbers. Richard Chessick observed borderline personality disorder widely among children—and the children he observed are now in their twenties. This is a disorder characterized by a "pervasive pattern of instability," lack of self-image and difficulty in forming interpersonal relationships.[3]

Borderline instability renders long-term goals difficult to achieve and causes marked mood shifts, anxiety, chronic feelings of boredom and emptiness. It is marked by uncertainty about important life issues, including sexual orientation, self-image and types of friends to have. Borderline people find it hard to be alone and will make frantic efforts to "avoid real or imagined abandonment."[4] Borderliners also feel "numbness" and depersonalization, especially during times of stress.

The root of borderline personality disorder is *abandonment*. It is now evident that sexual abuse also plays a role.[5] Suicide is far higher among borderliners than for the population at large.

Borderline personality disorder is widespread among Xers. Chessick is correct: it results from the "current whirlwind of barbarism."

As is the case with PTSD, borderline requires some kind of counseling or therapy as a step along the way to finding community, which is the ultimate remedy for abandonment. It seems that the third decade of life is a crucial period for treatment of this disorder. So twenty-somethings are of an age to begin treatment.

Another problem seemingly widespread among Xers, and which can be described and treated clinically, is identity disorder. The essential feature of this disorder is stress caused by inability to integrate different aspects of the personality into a coherent sense of one's self. Identity disorder makes it difficult to choose a life pattern, to form friendships or to make commitments. "Frequently the disturbance is epitomized by the person's asking, 'Who am I?' "[6] Identity disorder resembles, but exceeds in severity, the usual adolescent turmoil and questioning.

PTSD, borderline personality disorder and identity disorder are three clinically diagnosable and treatable problems that seem to be widespread among Xers. Of course, Generation X has among its members people who suffer from all the emotional problems and mental illnesses present in any age group. But these three seem worthy of special notice because American life today spawns them in profusion.

Borderline and identity disorders have a special affinity with the issues of trust connected with growing up today—which Janet, like so many others, found troublesome in her own childhood. As she noted, most Xers have the same questions but do not have the severity of emotional disturbance that would indicate a need for therapy.

A good rule of thumb I have found is to suggest counseling or therapy when emotional problems make it difficult to function in the daily routines of living. When a great deal of time and energy is consumed in just "holding it together," professional help is indicated. Rape, sexual or severe emotional abuse and exposure to life-threatening violence by their very nature indicate a need for professional expertise on the part of the counselor. A personal or family history of drug or alcohol addiction is a good indicator that a person would benefit from one of the Twelve-Step programs.

Because so many Xers do have one or more of the problems we have discussed, it seems the need for some kind of counseling, therapy or Twelve-Step work is extensive among young adults. We recommend as a first step talking over problems with a friend or older person with some experience. Begin the healing process in the community of friendship. If painful memories long buried begin to surface or if the "emotional baggage" becomes more disconcerting, then seek counseling—but continue the friendship. If you have no friends or mentors you can trust, then begin with a counselor. Meetings of AA or another Twelve-Step program are easy places to start because immediate understanding and acceptance are offered there.

Much of what we have said is ordinary common sense, but it must be stated because there is widespread misunderstanding both about the kind of problems people face and about the role of therapy or Twelve-Step programs. On the one hand, some people—men especially—are reluctant to seek any help whatsoever in working through their problems. On the other hand, some seem now to believe that everything is dysfunctional, everyone is a victim, and therapy or support groups are a necessary way of life. As is usually the case, wisdom is to be found between the two extremes.

Community Begins with a Friendship

In a culture like ours, where the individual is so dehumanized, the recovery of genuine humanity begins with the forming of real friendships. Friends genuinely care for one another. A friend does not "use" the other person to achieve some goal—for example, befriending only those coworkers who might enhance one's chances of promotion. Friends trust each other. For Xers who have learned not to trust anyone, friendship is a decisive step in the direction of healing— either of the generational lack of trust that Janet describes or of directly experienced trauma.

Friendship transports a person from concern for self to concern for another. Friends are willing to "bear one another's burdens." Friendship comes in different degrees and levels. One may have only a few very close friends over a lifetime. But there can be many others whom one does not know as well or even for very long with whom it is possible to establish a relationship of genuine trust and concern. Groups are effective in the healing process, because in a group one encounters others as authentic persons. Friendship of this kind might be transitory, but it is no less real. It can be a first step in the formation of other more lasting friendships. We have seen this often in young adult groups.

A person may choose to divulge the deepest hurts only to a counselor, but friendship enables one to "try again" in the business of building relationships. Through friendship, trust comes into being even where it did not exist before. In most cases friendship can serve as the most effective way of healing past hurts.

Janet's conviction that friendship is the most important healer is borne out by my experiences as a Vet Center counselor and by my years as a college chaplain and young adult pastor. Many times, in fact, I have seen friendship succeed when therapy failed. Though therapy and counseling continue to be important, there is a danger that they will become just one commodity among many that can be purchased in a consumer society—or a commodity that one cannot afford. So Generation X must work to restore friendship.

"Symptoms" in the Search for Meaning

We noted in the first chapter that people frequently mistake certain feelings, attitudes and perceptions of self for symptoms of clinical disorder. Some "symptoms" are really healthy reactions to extreme stress. This analysis was first made by Peter Marin writing about Vietnam veterans.[7] Marin believed that such "symptoms" as feelings of being scapegoated, guilt, inability to love and alienation from one's own feelings can be symptoms not of clinical stress but of *moral pain.*

What Marin wrote of Vietnam veterans is even more true of Xers in their reactions to life in the whirlwind of barbarism. "Symptoms," especially those that resemble the clinical symptoms of identity disorder, are really appropriate questions and attitudes arising from Xers' experience. Moral pain is a realistic and healthy reaction to a very disordered situation. It is a sign of mental health and indicates real insight.

Janet has identified the real nonclinical identity question of Generation X. It is not "Who am I?" Most Xers already know who they are. The true question, she believes, is "Who am I going to be?" This is a profoundly different question because it does not spring from self-doubt, lack of self-esteem or immaturity, but from a conviction that the world is so "out of joint" that one's future might well be foreclosed. This question is oriented legitimately toward the future. It does not arise from a troubled past but from awareness of a disordered and hostile world. Xers are asking the right questions.

To see these questions and the attitude that gives rise to them as clinical disorder is simply wrong. To use clinical categories to frame the questions is to rob the Xer life experience of its moral content and to mask the true nature of that experience. Xers are not merely survivors—they are attempting to refashion the world in response to their questions. In young adult communities the questions acquire a "we" dimension: "Who will we be together?" and even become political: "How will we change the world together?"

Therapists deal exclusively with *intrapsychic* issues: personal trauma and its healing. Our "psychologized" society, following its experts and gurus, also tends in this direction. Xers do not. They want *real* answers to *real* questions. They seem instinctively to know, even though many of them have never had it, that community is the place of real healing. Community is also a place where real change begins.

Therapy, while sometimes *necessary* for emotional well-being, is never *sufficient* for complete healing. The need for therapy in the high dosages we now seem to require originates in the breakdown of basic communities and the lack of true friendship. Restoration of community is the primary need for Generation X.

Moreover, the therapeutic emphasis on the individual's intrapsychic problems both results from and reinforces the excessive individualism of the late twentieth century. Therapy helps the individual to "adjust" and to "cope." It helps to "socialize" the individual. Xers banded together in groups and communities are a feisty bunch with a streak of downright "cussedness." They do not seem in any hurry to be socialized. They would rather "resocialize" the world, remaking it into a more therapeutic locale.

Xers who find healing in community discover a springboard out of self-absorption. Communities that Janet sees as pockets of resistance are indeed that. They are, in fact, subversive of the "me first" attitudes our society has come to espouse.

"Apathetic," "lazy," "Peter Pan" Xers pondering together what they and the world should become may indeed pose a threat to the status quo. To their credit, they seem to resist efforts to label them. They are unwilling to be tamed or domesticated.

Xers are unable to disconnect their sense of well-being and wholeness from the instinctive need for meaning. In the previous chapter we discussed the search for meaning. This has considerable bearing on the present discussion, for mental and emotional health are impossible apart from the perception that there is a coherent structure of reality.

A case has been made by the psychologist Viktor Frankl that the primary motivational force in life is the attempt to find meaning.[8] Frankl, a survivor of the Holocaust, differed from Freud, who located the source of motivation in the pleasure principle, and from Adler, who located it in the will to power. Generation X forces us to recognize with Frankl the importance of the fundamental human instinct for meaning and to acknowledge the disturbance that results when it is frustrated.

Psychology with its various therapies offers only tentative and partial support in the holistic healing for which Xers are searching. Authentic community affords much more. Both are incomplete, however, without a deeper grounding in a total worldview. The Xer quest for meaning and the need for healing are inseparable. Both become possible only when situated within the larger context that only faith provides.

The Role of Religious Experience
I have a friend who was abused as a child. As a young man, he served in the military. While in Vietnam he performed assassinations in

connection with CIA clandestine operations. He also tortured and killed prisoners. In the midst of carrying out torture and murder, he underwent a conversion experience reminiscent in some ways of the conversion of Saul of Tarsus into the apostle Paul. He is now a devout Christian. He has been through psychotherapy with good results, has been involved in veteran self-help groups and knows as much about the healing process as anyone I know. He is, in fact, frequently called upon to teach psychiatrists how to deal with evil.

Several years ago he spoke before a television camera about Vietnam and its residue of evil. He made a public statement that better describes the role of an encounter with God in healing the effects of evil than anything I have heard before or since. He said: "The kind of evil I have done and experienced is incredibly powerful. It is transcendent. There is only one power greater, one that transcends even evil of this magnitude. That is the power of God's grace."

My friend spoke not from any theoretical understanding—though he has that too—but from his personal experience. His comments are relevant to Xers because the afflictions they suffer in disproportionate numbers are not just problems to be solved or neuroses that can be "therapized." We have been talking in this book about real and enduring evil, monstrous and threatening.

Psychiatrists, therapists and counselors often have no idea how to deal with this kind of evil. Some of the more honest among them are coming to recognize this fact. For example:

PTSD patients frequently do not fare well when undergoing traditional forms of psychotherapy. . . . Surviving some type of trauma may be the first step in a lifelong struggle to reconstitute values, beliefs and a sense of meaning to life. . . . These issues often render traditional psychotherapy ineffective because spiritual and existential issues become paramount. . . . PTSD patients . . . must frequently deal with real moral misdeeds. . . . They may realize that they have committed, or been involved in, acts with real and terrible consequences. Often, then, their recovery must have a dimension (spiritual) that creates unfamiliar and/or unwanted territory for many therapists.[9]

The spiritual dimension that is unfamiliar territory to many therapists is—or should be—quite familiar to Christians. It is the terrain through which Jesus walked on the way to the cross. The final healing is that given to us in the risen Lord.

Some personal experience of this is crucial in healing aloneness. The shared experience of Jesus is a part of Christian friendship and of membership in the Christian community. The experience of Jesus, given to us by the Spirit, is the healing power of God's grace. It does not dispense with the need for counseling or recovery programs or friendship, but it pervades all of these. My Vietnam vet friend understands this. So does Tracey H.

The Story of Tracey H.

Tracey, a member of Generation X and a friend to both Janet and me, grew up in a very troubled home. Both parents were alcoholics. She was verbally abused and beaten by her mother. When she was fifteen, her mother told Tracey that she was not really her daughter by birth. As an occasional baby sitter in the neighborhood, her mother had been accustomed to taking in children for short periods of time. One day a woman had left an infant girl and never returned. The abandoned infant was Tracey.

Learning this, Tracey realized that her abandonment had involved *two* sets of parents. Crushed, she attempted suicide. Her attempt fortunately failed. But she struggled for years with a desire to kill herself. At the age of seventeen, determined to escape from her "mother," she joined the navy. She loved recruit training because it wasn't home. She began to do some serious drinking and soon became a full-fledged alcoholic.

During her navy career she tried marriage, but found that her husband was emotionally distant from her and was never really interested in her sexually. The marriage lasted for several years but then ended in divorce. After the divorce, her former husband wrote her a note explaining that for him their marriage had been simply an attempt to discover whether he was heterosexual or homosexual. It turned out he was homosexual.

Tracey realized that nothing was working for her, so she began to take steps to change her life. She underwent therapy, stopped drinking and went into a Twelve-Step recovery program. Both her therapy and the recovery program worked well for her. The healing process had begun.

But there was another side to Tracey. Her God space was very large and as yet unfilled. At the age of eleven Tracey had asked her mother to allow her to be baptized, and her mother had reluctantly consented. Tracey had attended church at least some of the time and found that God came in and out of her life. By the time she began her recovery from alcoholism, she found she had a capacity for friendship and made a few close friends within the Twelve-Step group. Her healing experiences now included therapy, a recovery group and friendship.

An important turning point came one evening when she was listening to a member of her AA group, a priest, talk about God. This man was able to speak of God not just as the "higher power" of AA. For the priest, as for Tracey, "God as I understand Him" was the God revealed in the gospel. That night the priest revealed to the group that once he started screaming at God, he realized that Jesus cried with him. That statement was for Tracey a moment of great grace. She was overcome by the awareness that "God was there all the time." She remembers, "I felt a sense of self-esteem I never had before. I realized I wasn't worthless."

When she looks back on her life from the vantage point of her late twenties, she realizes that her friendships in the recovery group were crucial for her. Through them she began to trust and to hope in the future. Tracey acknowledges the importance of her therapy, the recovery group and especially her friendships. But the final step, the completion, came with her personal experience of God's healing grace.

Tracey's story continues. She joined a parish congregation and our young adult community. Her Christian life had been "one continual Good Friday," but more than a year ago she remarked, "Now I understand the Resurrection." She describes her experience of the risen Jesus as "the death and resurrection in my own life. It is the death in me of wanting death, it is the death of feeling worthless and unwanted. Things still hurt, but they hurt differently. I now know that even though any one of my friends may fail me, God never will."

She understands the sequence of the Christian life. "At first," she says, "I clung to the cross because I thought that's all there was, but now I understand the joy of Easter and that through Christ I am deserving of that joy."

During her time of developing Easter joy, Tracey began to write songs and poetry, which she sang or read for the young adult community and for her parish congregation. Her poems are hymns of praise by an Xer to the God who healed her.

Though Tracey's story is unusual and the distance traveled on her spiritual journey remarkable, she is not untypical of Generation X. Her questions "Do I amount to anything?" and "Am I worthless?" resonate in a generation so alone that its characteristics can be described with reference to clinical disorders.

Nor is Tracey unique in the manner of her deliverance. Xers in abundance know all about the need for therapy, recovery programs and friendship. Like Tracey, and unlike many in older generations, most Xers can accept their need for this kind of help, and they are quite willing to help each other. There is, as we have noted, a certain humility in Generation X.

More to the point, in the risen Christ, Tracey has begun to find the answer to the question "Who am I going to be?" Her deep awareness of the Lord's resurrection and her subsequent transformation into an "Easter Christian" place her at the leading edge of her generation's spiritual journey.

The Easter Encounter of Generation X

Like Tracey, many Xers understand Good Friday better than any other part of their faith. As we noted in a previous chapter, traditional Christian words like *sin* and *guilt* must be used with caution among Xers because they lose their theological meanings and take on psychological connotations related to lack of self-esteem. Good Friday is a way of life, and the cross is all there is for them. This is not surprising, given the similarity of X's generational questions to the symptoms of identity disorder.

But Tracey and other Xers have already recovered and reclaimed their Christian faith and its very root. They have made personal the most ancient Christian proclamation: "Christ is risen." They have begun to experience the healing power of the new life that is the gift of the risen Lord.

Such an experience in no way diminishes the need for the other steps in the healing process, but it pervades and transforms the others. Healing of this kind cannot stop at the boundaries set by therapy with its goals of intrapsychic health. It transcends also the shallow "me and Jesus" spirituality found in certain strains of American Christianity. It simply knows no limits.

The Easter experience leads immediately to that of Pentecost and the sending of the Spirit, who continually renews in us and in the world what was done in Jesus. Easter spirituality ties together some central threads of biblical Christianity long neglected in the Western Church. It emphasizes that we are "heirs with Christ" and "children of adoption." We are "no longer servants but friends."

Western Christianity of the last five centuries has emphasized what we are saved *from*, rather than what we are saved *for*. It stresses the past rather than the future. Xers like Tracey emphasize something that is equally biblical but that has been largely lost from view—God is at work in me and in the world *now*, and God is calling us into the *future*.

That this emphasis has immense healing power was demonstrated to us one evening during a young adult retreat. We had invited a young Roman Catholic monk to speak to us on Saturday, after a barbecue supper on the beach. As a monk, he was an object of some curiosity. But as a fairly recent graduate of one of our local universities, he could relate to the group. He appeared to be in his late twenties, so he shared the generational concerns of his hearers. Moreover, he was a member of a minority ethnic group. He had been invited to speak on any topic he chose connected with his own life.

With the dinner fire still burning in the cool evening and the sound of waves breaking on the beach behind us, we sat in the sand to hear what this exotic person, garbed in his monastic robes, might have to say. He spoke to us from his heart about what we mean when we say that God is Father, Son and Holy Spirit—the Blessed Trinity. It was nothing new, all quite biblical, and what he said had been said before—most notably by Augustine in his great fourth-century work *On the Trinity*. But we were deeply moved—some to the point of tears.

He explained the 2 Peter 1:4 text "you . . . may become participants of the divine nature" in terms of our brokenness and the unspeakable dignity God bestows on us by this invitation to share as children of adoption in the very inner life of God.

During the period of conversation and questions after his talk, the floodgates burst and issues of sexual abuse, addictions, lack of self-esteem and pain came to the surface—as they always do. But the context of the issues was subtly altered, for the question was not how to create self-esteem from brokenness, but how to recognize the esteem God has for each of us and how to realize the unimaginable dignity and grandeur we already possess.

This Easter experience with its awareness of the ongoing Pentecost and its reach to our ultimate destiny and dignity as sharers of the divine nature speaks most deeply to Generation X. It best conveys the healing power of the gospel. The Easter experience is the final answer to Janet's question: "Who am I going to be?"

As the modern world continues to break apart its citizens, the postmodern people of God are reconstituted and healed of their aloneness by God who calls us as children of adoption and—most wondrously—makes us "participants" or "sharers" of the divine nature. As children of adoption, as sisters and brothers of Jesus, we are called to share in some way in the life of the Blessed Trinity—the Divine Community. As we are transformed by the power of that Community, all other communities again become possible. Spousal love, family, friendships, neighborhoods, the world itself: all are renewed.

Within this infinitely widened scope of redemption, our healing takes place at an accelerated rate. Each of us is now able to say to any assault upon our dignity or self-esteem what Paul said of death: "Where is your sting?"

5

PERSONAL RELATIONSHIPS

The Changing Family (Janet)

My friend and I talked quietly over lunch at a small table in the sunshine. She and her husband are thirty, and she is pregnant with their first child. She was rather overwhelmed—and not only with the morning sickness and random hormones. She was trying to make decisions about her career. How long should she take off work? Should she bother pursuing her promotion? Whom could she trust with her child while she worked? And should she go back to work at all?

For women of my generation, this is one of the most difficult decisions. They spend so many years earning degrees and working their way up that it seems absurd to simply stop. But it also seems absurd to them to have a child and leave it for someone else to raise. For a man to give up his career after ten years' employment in order to raise children would be considered economic suicide. But women with the same degree and same ten years' employment have the option of giving it all up—or paying a big portion of their salary to someone who can care for their children while they work. Neither is ideal.

Family life is changing, largely due to the changing roles of women, and Xers are both part of the change and caught in the middle. The change, though, is not limited to the roles of women. Because the women in Generation X have careers and spend less time at home, they are requiring their men to take a larger part in housework, cooking and childrearing. This generation of people are attempting a difficult task of creating entirely new roles for men and women—a task that is causing confusion and frustration for both. Our parents have offered us two different examples, that of a working dad and a housewife mom and that of two working parents. Neither of these models seems ideal. Xer women are equally as educated as Xer men and enjoy the impact they can make in the business world, but we also desire a closer family life than was common among our working parents. Can we have both?

Even women who grew up in happy, stable, traditional nuclear families are finding they want something different from the husband-wife mother-father examples they had. The dilemma for me and for women like my pregnant friend is that we know what we can do in the world. We know we can make a difference, and we like competing in the business world and being independent. But we also know that once we leave that world we will be replaced rather easily, but once we have a child no one can replace us as a mother.

Xer women were told by the women's movement of the generation before them that they could have a career and children just like a man—and that they should. What Xer men and women alike are discovering is that unless the roles of men change, either the career suffers or the family does. The men of Generation X are being strongly criticized by their female counterparts for not taking as much a part in home life as women are taking in the working world. Xer women are frustrated with the dual expectations Xer men are placing on them. Many men are placing nineties expectations of career on their spouses while largely retaining a fifties view of the wife-and-mother role. Consequently most women work as much as men outside the home but are still expected to do the majority of the housework, cooking, shopping and child care.

Women's equality has only come halfway. The sixties changed the women, but the nineties are changing the men.

The men of Generation X are the first generation to grow up with women as equal counterparts—in theory, anyway. In my junior-high school our class was the first to require boys and girls to take wood-shop *and* home economics. The Baby Boomers swore to raise their boys with the values of women's liberation, but confusion came when the boys were taught one example of manhood and saw another in the world. They were quite literally told to create new roles for men. They were told to be "sensitive" yet manly, an active father while a successful career man, a husband who does the dishes, assists in the birth of his children and knows how to treat a woman like a man and a woman at the same time. There are very few role models for this new type of man, yet Xer men are expected to be that way by Xer women. No wonder we are so slow to become husbands and wives and mothers and fathers. Instinctively we try to follow the examples of our parents, but the expectations we place on each other are vastly different.

Our attempt to change family roles has produced two different outcomes. First, we see men making a sizable contribution to child care, and it seems it is less out of compliance with women's demands and more because they simply want to. Many men have told us they are overjoyed that it is suddenly acceptable, encouraged and possible that they spend less time earning wages and more time raising their children.

Kathy and Chris are a good example of Xers raising children. Chris has arranged his schedule so that two days a week, while Kathy works, he is home with their son, Eric. Kathy is home with Eric two different days, and one day Eric stays with a baby sitter. This model of family is becoming more and more popular with my generation, for it seems to foster a closer family unit while allowing for both parents' involvement in the business world.

A less successful model of our attempts at family life is planned single parenthood. Childbirth to unwed mothers has more than doubled in the past twenty years, and in 1992 the largest increase in single motherhood was among college-educated career women. This not only reflects a change in moral standards but also makes some interesting statements about women's choices. Statistics have shown that many of these single mothers live just above or below the poverty level, and the fathers are unlikely to participate in the upbringing of the child. Why are women making these choices?

A great many factors contribute to the continuing rise in births to unwed mothers. Some women feel they have fought tooth and nail in order to gain financial independence and the last thing they want is to be dependent on a man. These women take the women's movement to heart uncritically, believing that being independent means relying on no one but themselves. Such a philosophy can only lead to a self-inflicted aloneness, and the women are often hoping to use a child to fill more than the child space.

The dramatic rise in teenage pregnancy has been startling, but often it is attributed to a similar aloneness. Countless young girls have felt neglected in single-parent homes with working mothers and want nothing more than a family. They want someone who needs them; they want their actions to mean something. Theirs seems a self-perpetuating cycle.

Similarly, the growth of street gangs can be attributed largely to children's having to live without a male role model. Children born to children often have no male role models except for the guy on the corner with lots of cash. The strength of street gangs lies in the fact that those men consider each other family. They "adopt" the younger boys and are often the main providers of food and clothing to the younger gang members. They fill the roles of fathers and brothers and are likely to provide the boys with a greater sense of family than they have ever felt before. It should not surprise us that they would live and die for their gang.

Changing Morals

The rate of single motherhood follows an upward curve of promiscuity. The stigma of premarital sex has all but disappeared, having been transferred to virginity. Statistics show that children are having sex earlier and with more people. Since the eighties we have known that sex can kill. My generation ought to be paralyzed by the fear of AIDS alone. But we aren't. Why *isn't* my generation being paralyzed by fear? Why is it that even though everyone knows how sex can kill, heterosexual intercourse has risen to number one on the list of ways the AIDS virus is transmitted?

People are educated about AIDS, but they are still needy, and I suggest that their need is less physical than emotional. The increase in reported AIDS cases and teen pregnancies has served as an indicator of promiscuity. From what I learn from men and women alike, what is most often desired from sexual encounters is affection. Love. Could it be that with all these broken homes and working parents, people simply do not get enough affection by traditional means? Could it be that they are simply seeking that affection from other people?

The most acceptable and readily available form of affection is that between a man and a woman. Sex, we are instructed on every billboard, in every movie, in every commercial, in every book, magazine, and matchbook cover, is a mandatory part of any male-female relationship, regardless of the level of commitment. Of course hormones allow us to heartily embrace that philosophy. But I think hormones take over when people seek out affection. I am not saying anything new, but I believe this explanation for the increase in teen pregnancies and sexually transmitted diseases (STDs) has validity. Promiscuity, STDs and teen pregnancies may be less a result of the sexual revolution than a symptom of a malnourished home life.

The Discipline of Trust

There is a way out of this dark tunnel in which Xers seem to be wandering. Xers are changing the family by creating new roles for men and women, but they are also creating a new type of family out of friends. I have heard it called "the New Family," and it consists of roommates, gang members or neighborhood children who are brothers and sisters for each other. Again, Xers are instinctively on a spiritual path, seeking out that which has been lost in recent years—trust.

A woman in her forties spoke to me about her Bible study group. She said, timidly, afraid to let down the barriers protecting her soul, that she had just that week really "shared" with her church group for the first time. The ice-breaker question "Who is your hero?" had been posed. She explained—very afraid of shocking me or making me think ill of her—that her hero was a man who had begun a church for drug addicts. What she liked best about him was that he had removed the cross from the altar. "The addicts understand all too well the crucifixion," she said; "he wants to emphasize the resurrection."

This level of sharing had terrified her. No one else in the group had ever opened up anything about their personal lives. They didn't think they could trust the others with what they really felt. And this was a *church group,* composed of Baby Boomers who likely grew up leaving their doors unlocked! How much *more* difficult trust is for those of us born into a world where you never talk to strangers and can't eat fruit given out at Halloween!

What Bill and I told this woman is the same thing we say to members of Generation X. You have to *practice* trust. It has to become a discipline like all others. The hard part for our friend was that she had to be the first one to trust the others—knowing that they did not trust her. And equally important, she had to first be *trustworthy.* She had to be what she wanted others to be—an example of trust.

As Bill mentioned earlier, we have reached a critical mass of people with low self-esteem; these people hardly consider trusting others, because they feel unreliable and untrustworthy themselves. And those who do find the courage to try are troubled by the dilemma of whom to place trust in. But Bill and I do see and encourage "pockets of resistance," where people come together in small groups to simply be with those they trust, with friends. Trust is a discipline that must be practiced, and we are finding that this discipline is bringing Xers together, out of the world and into friendship.

At the moment Xers are noted for their "flakiness," their reluctance to commit to marriage and career. In the future, however, Generation X will be remembered because of their friendships. The hope we see in Generation X lies largely in the importance they put on personal relationships. Xers are recapturing, slowly and in a new dimension, the foundation of friendships—and all friendships begin with trust.

Xers want to change the world, but they won't do it by standing on podiums and shaking their fists. They won't do it by linking arms and chanting slogans. They won't do it by shouting or dropping out or running for president. We Xers will change the world in a whisper— by changing the way we relate to one another as men and women, and as friends.

The Xer Dilemmas (Bill)

Anyone who works as a pastor or counselor to young adults knows of the anguish young women face over the motherhood-work conflict. The dilemma Janet describes hangs like a pall over Generation X. It affects both men and women, but in different ways. At stake are the most fundamental and intimate of personal relationships: male-female, family, parent-child, small communities.

Xer women seem less sure than their Boomer predecessors that you can successfully meet both the demands of motherhood and the increasing stresses of career. Having listened countless times to young women sorting out their options, I have come to believe that the conflict is almost universal and that it admits of no real resolution given the way society and the economy are now organized. Older women are now arriving at similar conclusions.

The other tangled path that Janet and her Xer peers must negotiate is the road that women and men walk together. Relationships between the sexes are never clear or completely defined, but we are now in the midst of real upheaval. The confusion of roles and expectations that Janet describes is pandemic.

I think Janet is correct in her belief that women have changed. My impression is that younger women are more sure of themselves and of their equality with men than were Boomer women in their twenties. In this Xers have benefited from the struggles of older women.

While they have been the beneficiaries of the feminist movement, increasing numbers of Xers are disavowing its more strident tones; they are assimilating feminism's insights and taking advantage of its gains, but placing it in a larger perspective.

Xer men, on the other hand, do seem more confused and less self-assured than were Boomer men in their twenties. Do you open a car door for a woman? Do you shake hands? Do you pay for a meal on a date, or do you split the cost? Is letting a woman go first an act of courtesy or condescension? Men no longer know what women want.

Although machismo prevails among a large segment of the Xer male population, twentysomething men are by and large more responsive than their elders to what women have been saying about equality and gender roles. But young men, knowing more about what women want for themselves, do not know what women expect of *them*. They are confused because women seem to want them to be both strong and masculine on the one hand and warm, sensitive and almost feminine on the other. The unanswered question is "How do you do this?"

So young men are stuck. Women want them to be more sensitive boyfriends and husbands—and certainly to be more involved as fathers—but their own fathers and older male mentors have provided little guidance.

Xer men and women are both caught in a particularly pernicious and hypocritical trap, in that society tells them they must be simultaneously productive and upwardly mobile in their careers, warm, sensitive, and affectionate in their relationships, and concerned, involved parents—and then offers them fewer jobs and demands of them longer working hours for less pay.

These dilemmas and confusions are so widespread among young adults that they necessarily set the agenda for Generation X. Though we elders now face some of the same issues, we did not spend our formative years and early adulthood trying to figure them out. The age at which a generation undergoes certain experiences sets its course for a lifetime. Generation X quite rightly places its primary emphasis on sorting out and redefining personal relationships.

We have no simple answers for these complex problems, but we believe that there are principles and perspectives that can serve as a basis for building relationships in a confusing time.

Sexual Promiscuity

Janet mentioned the sexual promiscuity rampant among her generation. This is indeed a significant problem, and one with ramifications for the future of marriage and family. Studies consistently show that people who live together before marriage have a higher divorce rate than those who do not. It seems also that habits of premarital sex incline people to postmarital adulterous affairs. Generation X did not begin the sexual revolution of the sixties—that dubious honor belongs to the Boomers—but Xers now live by the tenets of that revolution.

To be fair to Generation X, one must keep in mind several facts that at least partially explain the rise in promiscuity. The first is that until rather recently it was possible, and was even the norm, for people to graduate from—or drop out of—high school, get a job, get married at the age of eighteen and support a family on a single income. Now the economic and educational requirements of the culture require that people stay single much longer. A college degree is now a necessity for many jobs—and it takes longer to obtain a degree in many state universities. Further training after college is often required. The job market is terrible, and people stay longer at entry-level positions—if they can even get them. All of this contributes to the fact that large numbers of young people with quite normal hormonal urges are forced to stay single well into their late twenties. This does present a problem. That is not to say that we are biologically determined; still, no matter how much we psychologize sex, it remains rooted in biology.

The second factor is the Pill. Sexual restraint has always been difficult for youth—at least I and my contemporaries thought so as far back as our adolescence during the early fifties. Truthfully, the fear of pregnancy intruded upon many a passionate evening in those days—had there been a pill available, there would doubtless have been far more unmarried sex than there was. The Pill was developed as the Boomers were on the threshold of adolescence. The young Boomers took full advantage of this new option of separating sex from pregnancy, and the sexual revolution was inaugurated.

Another significant change is the public role of the Church. Until recently the Church played a major part in setting the moral tone of the culture. This is no longer true; the Church now inhabits the cultural periphery. Sexual restraint was more attainable in a culture that supported efforts at restraint. Sexual failure was frequent, but there was always repentance and grace.

Large numbers of Xers (and Boomers too) no longer have any church connection and see no significance in any Christian statement about the purpose of sex. Coinciding with the marginalization of the role of the Church has been a real decline in morality in all areas, including the sexual.

The only Xers I know who make any efforts at sexual restraint are members of Christian churches, young adult communities and campus fellowships who not only take Christian moral standards seriously but also sense some kind of intrinsic connection between physical sex and the deep personal and public commitment that mature sexuality entails. Of course, many people in older generations have never seen those connections and never will.

The price is very high for the members of Generation X who try to withstand the tide of promiscuity. Janet is correct in stating that virginity now bears the stigma once attached to premarital sex. The burden of explanation is now on the person who objects to a college roommate's having sexual intercourse in the bed on the other side of the room. The cultural norms of sexual morality have shifted 180 degrees in two generations. Xers didn't create the new standard, but they live by it. The cultural norm is now quite clearly that *all* romantic relationships are and must be physically, genitally sexual.

Society bought into the sexual revolution of the sixties. This was essentially an adolescent phenomenon, whatever spin is now put on it. Older Americans didn't like the revolution, but they offered no viable alternatives, shared little of the sexual wisdom they should have acquired and eventually accepted the new mores themselves. And so we became a nation fixated at the level of adolescent sexuality.

This brings me to the "Lech Walesa theory of morality." The hero of the Polish revolt against the communist regime commented about that system: "A fish rots from the head down." In the case of changed sexual behavior, the head of the rotten fish is clearly to be found not among Xers but among the older generations.

Sexual promiscuity is fostered by the example of sexually irresponsible elders. It is enshrined by the pornography that pervades our television screens and by the tenor of commercial advertising. Generation X does not run these institutions. Xers, raised on the notion that safe sex and condoms are a viable substitute for restraint, can hardly be expected to be pioneers of sexual morality. Never in history has youth, engulfed as youth always is in the flow of hormones, been inclined to sexual restraint. Young people cannot be expected to set the moral norms and standards of sexual behavior, but older people can be expected to exercise some responsibility over the institutions they run.

But the rot has spread to Generation X, and they must now assume personal responsibility for some of it. The 60 percent increase in out-of-wedlock births during the 1980s is largely the doing of Xers—with some help from younger Boomers.

Epidemic out-of-wedlock births indicate a society in which real affection and trust between the sexes have eroded and concern for children has vanished. Xers may have inherited this society, but the responsibility for changing it now lies with them for the simple reason that they are in the prime fertility zone.

Issues for Men

Xer women are concerned about their men, and in moments of candor, young adult males will admit the concern is well placed. The issues discussed at the beginning of this chapter perplex us all, but Xer men are much more confused than women. Hence a section on men.

The specific problem we have in mind is the confusion and turmoil surrounding the meaning of masculinity in a world that now demands of men an almost feminine sensitivity. Women want men to resolve this issue. I occasionally hear a young woman blame something a male has done or said on "testosterone poisoning." Further inquiry reveals that the man has done something she considers insensitive. I have even been permitted to sit in on group discussions about the issue, and I am happy to report my findings.

When women talk about "testosterone poisoning," they are referring in one way or another to male aggression. I believe the men of Generation X, though presently confused by the turmoil we have described, are actually better situated than men of previous generations to liberate both themselves and women from the horrible burden of male aggression. This is the case because Xer men are more sensitive to women's reactions.

The good news is that twentysomething women are not interested in the "unisex" male advocated by some of the more strident forty-something feminists. Xer women frankly admit that they like, enjoy and expect some of the more exuberant manifestations of testosterone. I am also happy to report that there isn't any bad news. The message is that we men have to rid ourselves at last of some traits, habits and attitudes we've been carrying around for a long time. None of us now living created the problem. We inherited it. Now's the time to change—and change we must.

Reports of surveys published during the past few years indicate, for example, that surprising numbers of men would rape a woman if they were in no danger of being caught. Many men still believe a woman owes them sex if they take her to dinner. The male tendency toward violence has not been eradicated in Generation X. The gang violence that is tearing our cities apart is the doing of Xer males. While Xer men in larger numbers are more receptive and open to the feminine perspective than are older men, they must still confront the violence within.

The world is now awakening to the millennia-old plight of women who have been in bondage and slavery, used for male gratification, raped, abused and saddled with the sole burden of childrearing. This awareness is good, necessary and long overdue. But Xer men need not bear the guilt for all that has happened to women. They are not the appropriate targets of the accumulated anger of older women— or of the jealousy of older men. Nor are they responsible for exploiting women in the workplace. Let the elders pontificate solemnly over these questions and hurl mutual recriminations. Xers are responsible not for the tangled and troubled past, but only for working out the male-female equation under present conditions.

The men of Generation X are primarily responsible to the women of their generation and to the children who will be their offspring.

They need to be lovers, partners, friends and parents together—and discover together how to do it.

Male Sexuality and Aggression

The most significant affliction we men impose on women is turning loose on them our misplaced aggression. Whether the roots of male aggression are biological or cultural is endlessly debated. The answer is probably both. But the practical fact of the matter is that men tend toward physical expression of aggression more than women do.

Male aggression serves a useful purpose—more evident in earlier times, when physical survival depended on it, than now in the age of computers and sedentary occupations. Aggression's more dangerous aspects must be examined and redirected.

Some would persuade us that all aggression among young boys should be checked because there is a continuum between rough play in boyhood and lethal combat in adulthood. To halt the latter, they say, stop the former. I disagree. There is a qualitative difference between the two. Aggression should be continually rechanneled and redirected but not denied. The neighborhood boxing champion can, with some guidance, develop sensitivity to others. The neighborhood drive-by shooter cannot. Physically demanding sports and other outlets are important for young males who desire them. So are consistent guidance and direction.

Parental guidance and the influence of elders, especially older males, is crucial in determining the outcome of aggression in young males—but men are increasingly absent from the lives of boys. Xer men must take full advantage of the nascent movement among men to be more involved in the home.

Xer males have been desensitized and socialized into violence by exposure to pornographic levels of it on television and film. This kind of vicarious violence continues the macho mystique and ensures that male aggression will continue to tear apart our society.

We tend to become what we do and what we see. Feminists know this and rightly advocate the entry of women into all sorts of fields, including those that require a good deal of assertiveness. Xer women seem to have learned this and can be assertive and aggressive without diminution of the sensitivity usually associated with women. They have feminized aggression. Xer men have not yet learned how to masculinize sensitivity.

We learn by doing. Men learn sensitivity not by denying anything within their own masculine constitution—including aggression—but by practicing sensitivity. Gentleness and the redirection and softening of aggressive tendencies can be learned through practice.

I know from my extensive work with veterans—and that now includes Xer veterans of the Persian Gulf War—that even violence unleashed without restraint in the killing rage of combat can be healed. War is, after all, the most macho pursuit of all, the most testosterone-poisoned human venture. (American women are limited to combat missions aboard ship and in aircraft, activities that do not turn loose the dogs of war with the same intensity as ground warfare.) If the healing of violence can occur among those who have committed atrocities, assassination, rape and murder, it can take place in anyone.

The lessons learned from my work with veterans are three. First, violence can and must be redirected.

The second lesson is that all violence has moral and religious dimensions, for it always requires either ethical justification or forgiveness. Violence ruptures relationships so profoundly that it calls into question the very existence of the "God space" within us or, alternatively, impels us into that space.

The third lesson is that women play a central role in the healing of violence. Violence destroys something at the very center of the soul. It kills the deepest sensitivities. The only way to bring about a "new life" is to entrust one's deadened humanity to another person. Our differentiated sexuality inclines men to want to do this with women, but there is a terrible fear that a woman will not understand and will reject the offering of one's deadened self. I cannot count the times

I have watched a man entrust to a woman his fear that he is "only an animal" and tell of his past crimes and enduring fixation on violence. And I have seen the restoration of full humanity when a woman forgives, accepts, understands and, quite literally, gives him back his life. It begins with trust.

Suggestions for Men and Women

I would not presume to offer younger men a specific set of guidelines and "how-tos" in this most intimate area of life, their relationships with women. I am, after all, not a member of Generation X, but an observer and friend. It seems, though, that certain tendencies implicit within male sexuality truly mesh with the feminine. These are present in us men and may be either activated or repressed. The men of Generation X, though they may be somewhat confused about their role with respect to women, are probably closer to disfranchising machismo than were men of earlier generations. Xer men are now free to become more liberated than we elders have been from the curse and bondage of violence. I believe we yearn to be free of it. From a Christian perspective, "For freedom Christ has set us free" (Galatians 5:1).

At every step of the way, men need attitudinal checks and feedback from women. The line between "testosterone poisoning" and appropriate male behavior can be learned in great part by listening to women with both heart and head, taking them very seriously as persons, companions and equals.

What is called for is, as we shall see, a "discipline of listening in trust" and a "sacramental" listening. Of course, this kind of attention to each other always must be mutual and reciprocal between men and women. But I can speak only from the masculine experience, and I think men find it especially difficult to listen from the depth of our souls. We must learn a different style, one that seems at first most feminine. For men it is important to be open, passive and attentive to women. I believe the real completion of male sexuality occurs when it acquires this kind of affinity for the feminine.

The women to whom Xer men should listen are not the feminist elders who seem to have little understanding of the male experience and who have encouraged women to become aggressive in a male way, but Xer women, their own contemporaries. Let Boomers work out their problems in their own way.

So, men, ask women with affection and respect what it is they want from you. Whether you do or do not hold the door for them, pay for dinner or suggest what to do on a date, do everything with the utmost respect and the kind of joyful affection that best expresses our differentiated sexuality.

Mutual affection and respect are, now as always, the key to the relationship between the sexes—and ultimately to all relationships.

Male and Female Sexuality

Sexuality, male and female, has a dimension that is seldom mentioned in the current public discussion. Though commonly thought to be a feminine characteristic, this dimension is intrinsic as well to full masculinity. It is a quality based on trust, and it resembles the ultimate and radical Godward stance that we will discuss in the final chapter of this book. I am speaking of the ability to surrender in faith and with great trust to another person.

This is not surrender in the sense of *giving up,* but a *giving over* of oneself to another with joy and exuberance. In this kind of surrender, power is returned to the giver—not power *over* another but power *from* another. Though this kind of language is especially appropriate to marriage, it has application to all relationships.

Most Xers, as was the case in preceding generations, will eventually marry or have a serious relationship. It is well to let the biblical ideal influence the entire sexual dimension and then flow over into other relationships. In this dimension, we enter first into trust and then into the experience of "mystery."

Again: The Discipline of Trust

Because trust is the basis of all relationships, and because trust is especially hard to come by in the conditions under which Generation X has lived, the development of trust cannot be left to happenstance. Janet's idea that trust must become a spiritual discipline is absolutely right. Just as an athlete or musician must spend hours practicing and building competence, people must work and practice to acquire the skills necessary for living. Trust is an enduring habit of mind and heart, acquired through relationships with people who are trustworthy. If trust is not developed through the early formative experiences in life, one can begin to develop it later by trusting others who are in fact loving and caring people. Trust is formed only in relationship with others.

If I find it difficult to trust, I must choose at least one specific person, or perhaps several, and *decide* to trust. The selection must be a careful one. I must then choose times, places and specific circumstances in which to share something of myself. I must keep on doing this over and over until the experience becomes part of my life.

Sometimes circumstances almost force us to trust others. This has been the case with me several times. I remember the fear I felt walking into a classroom for the first time as a teacher of college seniors. I was in my midtwenties, only slightly older than my students and afraid I couldn't do the job adequately. I trusted my students to let me be their teacher. They did. In Vietnam I entrusted my life on several occasions to my nineteen-year-old chaplain's assistant. He was worthy of the trust. I entrusted myself, with some initial fear, to a woman with whom I fell in love—and she entrusted herself to me. That trust has by now blossomed into an eighteen-year marriage.

Through trust, friendship becomes not only possible but actually one of the joys of life. Personal relationships of all kinds enrich us. For those who choose the commitment of marriage, trust brings genuine, mature, full, reciprocal and joyous sexual intimacy. This enduring way of being will then become the couple's gift to their children.

Even if one has grown up in a nurturing and loving environment, trust must still be a spiritual discipline because it is so easy to become hard, to withhold oneself from others, in a hostile culture such as ours.

Trust as a spiritual discipline is akin to prayer as a spiritual discipline—and for the same reason. Prayer—direct, intimate conversation with God—must become an intentional part of our daily routine. Otherwise the busyness of life tends to choke out time with God. It is very easy to fall out of the habit of prayer and lose one's daily intimacy with God. Saints and mystics, Christian writers and spiritual directors have told us this for centuries. The contemporary Christian agenda is full of sermons, books and suggestions on how to develop the discipline of prayer.

A married couple, caught up in work and in raising children, frantically trying to keep up on the treadmill of daily living, must program times they will spend only with each other—they must discipline themselves to do this. Without the experience of being together, the marriage withers and dies. Parents must spend time—large amounts of time—with children, especially when they are young. This requires tremendous discipline.

These are things "everyone" knows. But we remain neglectful. The counseling industry thrives because husbands, wives and parents do not continue their efforts. In most areas of life, it seems, we must pay more attention to the formation of good habits through the practice of self-discipline.

Mystery

Both Hebrew and Christian Scriptures assume a holistic approach to life. Neither Jews nor the earliest Christians could separate body from mind, emotion from thought—it took later Western philosophy to do that.

In the biblical perspective the inner and outer dimensions of life are inseparable. Social-individual and physical-spiritual are simply different facets of the same reality. Similarly, one's relationship with fellow humans (and with the earth) and with God are inseparable.

Needless to say, this biblical outlook is a casualty of modernity. Postmodern Xers may recover it by following their inclination to seek the personal, by deepening their emphasis on relationship, friendship and community. Generation X has rediscovered a great truth: in interpersonal exchanges—especially at the deeper levels—there is something of the mysterious, the undisclosed, the partially hidden. We are drawn out of ourselves and into another person in a way we can never describe in words, nor even fully understand.

In a marvelous exchange with us, God, our Creator takes on our own flesh in the person of Jesus: "The Word became flesh . . ." God, who is essentially beyond our comprehension, is now revealed to us in the person of Jesus, who mingles with us, sharing life, suffering and even death with us, so that we might share in his victory over death. By this act, humanity is now elevated beyond anything we could dream. We now realize the fullness of our creation in the image of God by being "conformed to the image of his Son" (Romans 8:29). There is a reciprocity between us and God that is given through Jesus. This was God's intent from the beginning, but is now revealed.

Paul writes of this as "the mystery that was kept secret for long ages but is now disclosed" (Romans 16:25-26). Paul wants the Colossians to "have the knowledge of God's mystery, that is, Christ himself, in whom are hidden all the treasures of wisdom and knowledge" (Colossians 2:2-3).

The Greek word Paul uses for "mystery," a word that is used throughout the New Testament to describe this great reality, is *mysterion*. This translates into Latin as *sacramentum* and into English as "sacrament." The Greek word does not have the modern English connotation of "mysterious" or unsolved problem or knowledge withheld, as in a murder mystery. The New Testament meaning is "that which, being outside the range of unassisted natural apprehension, can be made known only by Divine revelation, and is made known in a manner and at a time appointed by God, and to those only who are illumined by his Spirit. . . . Its Scriptural significance is truth revealed."[1]

God's intent for humanity is revealed fully and physically in Christ Jesus. The inaccessible God, creator of a universe of countless galaxies, has made known his general purposes through creation, spelled them out in history to the people of Israel and has now become intimate with us physically in the person of Jesus. We are able to understand that God is a God of love and of reconciliation only because of the physical presence of God in Christ.

Paul carries this even further. He picks up an Old Testament theme that the love of husband and wife resembles that of God and his people (Hosea 2). He reapplies it by comparing the love of husband and wife to the love of Christ and the Church. What can be said of one can be said of the other. In a remarkable passage—Ephesians 5:21-33—he uses the same word, *mystery*, to apply equally to both loves and both relationships.

Paul says essentially that if you want to understand the love of Christ and the Church, the closest human expression possible is the love between spouses. Spousal love is the best way to catch a glimpse of God's love. It goes the other direction too: if you want to know the full potential of the sexual intimacy and all that marriage entails, look to the person and the work of Jesus. Look especially to the complete self-giving of Jesus on the cross, and look at the gift of the new life in the risen Lord. Then look to the self-giving of your spouse. These are, in the Christian perspective, inseparable from one another. Many of us who are married can attest to the truth of Paul's statement—I certainly can. Marriage to Carol has provided me with my deepest intimations of God's love.

The New Testament is filled with passages that expand on this theme and apply it to other relationships. Examples: There is such close identification between God and his people that Jesus says that what is done to a fellow human is done to him (Matthew 10:40; 25:40).

Saul of Tarsus was on the road to Damascus so that he might persecute the followers of Jesus, but the risen Lord asked him, "Why do
you persecute me?" (Acts 9:4). The first and great commandment is
to love God, but the second is like it: "Love your neighbor as yourself"
(see Luke 10:27). Jesus prayed that we might be one with each other
and with him even as he and the Father are one (John 17:20-21). The
love we have for God and our love for each other are inseparable (1
John 4:7-21).

Sacrament in its most ancient historical meaning refers to the work
of Jesus, who is the visible sign of God's presence in the world. The
term was then applied to the Church, the "body of Christ." We know
from Scripture that Christ is the head of the body and we are its
members, each with different gifts (1 Corinthians 12; Ephesians 1:22;
Colossians 1:18). The Church is an outward and visible sign of the
inward and spiritual grace given to the world in Jesus.

The word *sacrament* in later centuries became restricted to the physical signs and symbols by which this grace becomes present to wor-
shipers in the Eucharist or Lord's Supper, in baptism and in other
sacramental rites. In all uses of the word, the underlying notion is that
God is present and active in the world in and through physical realities and external things—first in the body of Jesus, then in the
Church, and finally in signs and symbols entailing the use of water,
bread, wine and the spoken word. God, in other words, does not
retreat from physical things into the internal world of ideas and emotions. Quite the contrary: physical realities are the bearers of God's
grace and the signs of his presence.

All relationships are thus in some way sacramental, because human
interchange is an echo and a reflection of the intimacy God intends
to have with us. The vastly complex network of human relationships
with different levels and nuances is connected to our intimacy with
God. Our love for one another is a mirror image of our love for God.
If we do not love our neighbor, we do not truly love God, for we love
God *through* our neighbor. This biblical message, though obscured in

our time, retains its extraordinary power.

Generation X, with its emphasis on the personal, is on the verge of rescuing this great truth from the brambles of a culture that has choked it out. Xers could reveal to us anew in very practical ways the implications of this great disclosure of God.

Sacramental Psychology

Xers who incline toward a gentler community life with more emphasis on interpersonal relations than now exists in the larger society are on the verge of a sacramental sense. Quiet, tolerant, gentle listening to another with empathy becomes habitual. It encourages disclosure of the previously undisclosed facets of the other.

The option of nihilism, the finding of no meaning or purpose in a hostile world, which is one direction Generation X could take, becomes quite unlikely in a world of sacramental awareness. The God-given purpose of all things and of all people, oneself included, unfolds gradually in and through daily experience. The discovery of God, linked so closely to the disclosure present in all human encounters, renders nihilism impossible.

Janet's belief that Xers are already "halfway there" in their search for God is verified in the sacramental way many of them go about establishing relationships and forming community. Xers dislike and disregard ideologies that attempt to define and limit interpersonal exchanges. They are beginning to break free of the intellectual constraints of modernity which have reduced human persons to objects— and they act on the basis of their intuition. Xers are, I believe, at least potentially a "sacramental generation." Their approach to the mystery that is always hidden and yet disclosed in Christ begins with their heightened awareness of the mystery that is to be found in each of us. They have some affinity for Jesus, who told his disciples: "I do not call you servants any longer. . . . I have called you friends" (John 15:15). Generation X is beginning to fashion a very practical sacramental psychology.

For Xers this is not a mere abstraction. Many try to live this way. The story of two young women whom I will call Alice and Jenelle illustrates this. Alice fell in love with a young man in her church group. He already had a girlfriend who was also in the group but he was immediately attracted to Alice and broke up with the other young woman, Jenelle. Alice was amazed to find that Jenelle was able to overcome her deep hurt, be reconciled to her and even become a friend.

Some time later, Alice's new love moved out of state and broke up with her by mail. Now she was the one who suffered. Aware of Jenelle's spiritual depth, Alice turned to her for help. In the "sacramental awareness" that permeated their friendship, they discovered new dimensions of our Lord's call to mutual forgiveness and reconciliation. This sacramental transaction took place within the very earthy domain of the aftermath of romantic love and sexual attraction.

Sensitivity to the sacramental dimension is implicit within human consciousness, but it must be cultivated. Janet's "discipline of trust"—actually practicing trust, just doing it—is the only way to develop awareness of sacramentality in relationships. Relationships in our culture are increasingly functional—people are defined by what they do. Sacramental spirituality counters this, for, like the Easter experience, it is open to the future. It awaits further disclosures, both from the other person and from God.

The discipline of sacramentality requires each of us to be conscious of who we *are*. To do this we must simply stop and contemplate other persons.

So stop, ponder and enjoy someone. Spend some quiet time reflecting on the qualities, foibles included, of any other person, especially one you care for. Do nothing. Just *be* in the presence of another. Simply enjoy, for you are in the presence of another human person and in the presence of God! That is the practice of sacramental awareness.

6

CHANGING
THE WORLD

Why Xers Will Change the World (Janet)

We Xers are not yet sure what political or economic changes we will bring about. As a generation we are too young to effect much political change except by casting votes, and we are just beginning to have the buying power that might lead to change in economic trends. At first glance we look like a muddled group with no real knowledge of where we should go, how we should get there or even why we would prefer one destination over another. We have not bound together with a cause, but we know we want *something* to change.

Every generation has its ideological youth who grumble over the way things are, reject the ways of their elders and are propelled by their desire to do things differently. This is the essence of youth. This youthful energy for change has caused nations and peoples to move forward since the beginning of time.

The difference between the youth of Generation X and all others before them is where we are beginning. It is not a matter of directly changing a political or economic system. We put little stock in the present systems, because we find them fundamentally wrong in that they treat people as commodities.

Every generation, every group of people, has its share of greed, individualism, corruption and evil. Generation X is not exempt. But what people of all ages are seeing when they look out their windows is that greed, individualism, corruption and evil are necessary components to maintain the "me first" lifestyle. These traits have recently made nations, companies and individuals rich and powerful. Generation X has been raised in a world that lauded these traits as "good for business."

The problem is that the effects of this school of thought do not end in the boardroom. This outlook has become a general way of perceiving others and has been the single largest factor in the breakdown of our society. When we stop respecting the person standing before us, we are proclaiming that life has no value. And when we devalue life, we necessarily devalue ourselves.

Our political and economic systems are based on the values, beliefs and priorities of the people who create them. It is here where we will see the biggest change caused by Generation X. In our attempt at change we will not aim for the head of the beast, but for its toes. Our leaders have little interest in governing this system with these values. We are in the process of changing our own values, beliefs and priorities. It is this process that will eventually change the world.

Through its devaluation of present social systems, our generation is learning to place more value upon people than on material objects. We are learning that in order to pour back into the world the dignity that has been drained from it, we must value the lives of others above anything that we might do, have or be. We are learning this slowly, and this belief system is spreading person by person, as the priorities of this new age of people are changing.

Generation X will change the world by placing more emphasis on personal relationships. We will change the world by reveling in and emphasizing our increasingly rich composite of ethnic backgrounds. We will change the world by changing the roles of men and women, in such a way that the distinctions between the roles will blur and mesh so we can work better together in the family and in business. We will change the world by changing what our children believe, and our elders will not quite recognize that change until they look out their windows one day at our children and realize that we have in a new, yet solidly familiar way, given each other dignity.

How Xers Will Change the World (Bill)

As we have seen, the feature that most distinguishes Generation X is the collective emotional, familial and social deprivation that leads to its characteristic aloneness. This in turn has led Xers to become primarily seekers of relationships, friendship and community. By moving in this direction, X becomes a "reactive" generation, because it sets a radically different course from that of its predecessors and defines itself against them. This generational tendency, as we shall see, has enormous implications for the world's future.

Because Xers grew up and were socialized in a period of moral, familial and social decay, two things happened to them. First, they acquired many of the characteristics of the society that formed them, but, second and more important, they have been so "burned" by the formative forces in their lives that they ultimately reject them and set out in a fundamentally new direction. They fight a battle within themselves between the values they assimilated and were taught and the values that their gut instincts tell them will fill the vacant spaces in their hearts. Among Xers the pull toward personal relationships is so powerful that it has become their generational defining characteristic. We predict that it will prevail over every other inclination.

We have already stated our belief that X is the first truly postmodern generation, coming to maturity as the modern era caves in under the weight of its materialism and unbridled individualism. It seems at present that everyone and everything is for sale. Human persons, now only another commodity, are being replaced by technology. The world, especially its economic system, is not "people-friendly." Nor is it family-friendly. Society has become me-centered and me-crazed.

Quite simply, Generation X, having suffered at the hands of this kind of society, is determined that the world will become more people-friendly and *we-centered*. Each generation has its turn at controlling society's institutions—the facts of aging and death ensure this. Xers are still too young to have had their chance, but their time is coming; and the generational characteristics we perceive among them indicate that the postmodern world they will guide into being will be a much different place.

Paradoxically, though Xers seem to care little about changing the world on a grand scale, their emphasis on friendship, community and noncompetitive alternatives flies in the face of the individualism and narcissism they learned growing up. It also defies the logic of the marketplace and the political system. But Generation X has learned the hard way that the system doesn't work and community does. Xers are *radicals* in the original meaning of that word, which translates roughly as "people who go to the root." They are quietly beginning to uproot the present system by creating an alternative.

Predictions are always dangerous, but, based on Generation X's defining characteristics, here are some of the ways we think Xers will impact and modify the social institutions they inhabit and will eventually run.

Family Life and Work

Remember, the Xer impulse is always to "rehumanize," to render the social environment once again habitable—beginning with their own marriages and their own children. The family is the institution most at risk in America, and Xers intend to turn the tide right on the home front.

Trapped, as are most Americans, in the economic stagnation that began in 1973 but has since worsened, virtually all Xer men and women *must* work outside the home. Working mothers are simply a fact of life for Generation X—but so are notions of equality between the sexes and the altered relationships between men and women, with men desiring and women expecting more male involvement in child-rearing and family. Xers, by the pressures they exert within their work situations, will ensure that the marketplace becomes more family-friendly.

Jane and her husband provide an example how Xers—without intending to do more than make their lives more bearable—are becoming agents of change. Both Xers, Jane and Paul knew they wanted children—eventually. Both worked hard and managed to save a little money along the way as they positioned themselves to ensure (as much as one *can* be sure of anything in today's job market) some career security. Jane chose a job with some flexibility, knowing that someday she would need it because she wanted to spend time with her future children.

As Jane worked her way up on the job, however, she encountered a problem: *she was a woman.* Along with other women in her workplace, she was paid less than men with similar positions.

Jane, truly a woman of Generation X, decided that she would gamble her career for a matter of justice. She did her homework, compiled figures on relative pay and confronted her boss—and his boss, and up the line. Jane won her battle—and because of her courage, so did the other women in her company.

When Jane became pregnant, she decided on the amount of leave she needed, not only for the last weeks of pregnancy but also for the first months of her child's life. She also decided on the kind of flexibility she needs in her future work schedule. Her company, aware that she has a good bit of fight in her, yielded to her requests. At the time of this writing, Jane is in the last month of her pregnancy. She and her husband are delighted with the immediate prospect of parenthood. They know the future will be difficult, but they are convinced they will succeed.

Jane and her husband have no illusions that they can "have it all." Jane has limited her career goals so that they are compatible with her desire to raise her child herself and do it the way she wants to. Jane and Paul have found what they think is a workable balance between work and childrearing. They will both have to work throughout their lives, and they intend to be productive at their jobs, but other personal values come first. Neither will tolerate job discrimination against women, nor will they allow anything to take priority over being parents.

Jane and Paul are tough-minded and courageous but sensitive, compassionate members of Generation X. Their struggles are paradigmatic for Xers—and so is the way they confront life.

Xers Won't Eat So Many Dogs

The economy is clearly a "dog-eat-dog" affair, but an economy driven by Generation X will be different, because they simply won't eat as many dogs. The familiar market-driven economy has now given place to a market-driven *culture* in which people are subordinate to the demands of the marketplace. A Darwinian survival of the economic fittest is the way things work now. Xers, with their focus on personal relationships, are likely to reverse this trend.

The generation that bore the brunt of the Depression in its youth and young adulthood was so conditioned by that experience that it built a postwar economy based upon material well-being. Now in old age, that generation will not, perhaps cannot, relinquish economic control or sacrifice material benefits for the sake of younger generations. The G.I. generation's commitment to materialism is one of "principle" and is unyielding. Xers, on the other hand, will tell you they want material success *so that they can pursue other, more important goals*—such as being with family and friends. This is an old value reintroduced to our postmodern world by a generation who never knew it growing up.

For many older Americans the economy as it has evolved is a given, a game that must be played by its own rules and for its own sake. Xers see it as a game to be played by *their* rules, as a system that must be beaten for the sake of other, more important values. For this reason, we are confident that Xers are embarked on a course that will change the economy in ways that are far less "dog-eat-dog."

Combining this trait with their other well-known commitments—to equality between the sexes and among the races, and their sensitivity to ecological concerns—we can venture some general predictions about the world according to Generation X.

All systems, economic, political and social, will have a more ethnically and racially diverse leadership shared by men and women. Cars will be more fuel-efficient, and regions that depend on the automobile will be forced to develop efficient public transportation—mostly out of the need to conserve energy, but also to meet demands from a very ecologically aware generation. Serious efforts and economic priority will be given to efforts that reduce pollution of the waters and of the atmosphere. There may be more concern for safety in the workplace, as Xers will reverse the tendency to sacrifice workers' safety to profit.

Some of these predictions reflect the continuation of trends already tentatively and precariously under way. Generation X did not originate the tendencies toward humanizing the world's institutions and preserving its environment, but Xers will make a generational commitment to enshrining them as the norm and standard for the postmodern era.

Quietly and Without Fanfare

Generation X does not have a conscious desire to change things on a grand scale. As Janet says, they aim for the toes rather than the head of the social monster. Nor do Xers tend toward grandiose public statements, as did Boomers, about the way things ought to be. They will utter only a whisper of the way things ought to be. Xers, as sharp and insightful as their elders, assume their place in the world quietly and go about their business without much notice, but they do make changes. Jane provided us one example. Mike gives us another.

Mike worked his way through college and thought he had finally graduated, but discovered after the graduation ceremony that the university did not accept some of his credits toward the degree. With graduate school in mind for the future, Mike went from part-time work to a full-time job and squeezed in the remaining classes wherever he could. This delayed the completion of his degree requirements, but he had no choice.

Mike went to work in a paralegal position and soon discovered two things. First, lawyers don't always operate according to legal ethics. The second discovery was more personal. His attorney bosses wanted him to work long hours, accomplish increasingly difficult tasks and accept little pay. He finally left in disgust and took a job with a large retail company. There too he discovered that he was expected to work long hours for as little above minimum wage as the traffic would bear.

Mike is a realist and looks on paid work as the only means to a very necessary end—providing money for food and lodging. His wife, who does not have a college degree, is similarly exploited by her employer. During their three years of marriage, one has often worked days, the other nights. Despite the obstacles, they have decided to focus on their marital bond and have succeeded quite well.

Because Mike is very competent, he soon rose to a supervisory position that paid a little more. Having been a leader in his college fellowship, he became knowledgeable in the problems of his fellow Xers, knowing they were his as well. Quite early he developed a critical attitude toward the shortcomings he feels are prevalent within his generation.

He was always critical of his agemates who were unable or unwilling to perform classroom or work assignments. He agrees with employers and workplace supervisors who despair over young adults' ability or willingness to fulfill minimum standards, to be on time or even to show up for work. Mike is aware of the reasons many of his fellow Xers operate this way, but he doesn't condone the behavior.

He is upset by the fact that fellow employees around his own age seem to have little sense of integrity, interest in their work or competence performing it. Their attitudes, he thinks, are destructive of their own future.

Now that Mike is in a supervisory position, he has begun forming friendly relationships with the Xers who are under him and venturing to give guidance and direction to some of them. He never attempts to motivate them by instilling loyalty to the company, because he has no more loyalty than they do to a corporation that cares nothing for its employees. Instead, he tries—with some success—to engender a spirit of personal commitment to one another among the employees. He encourages them with what he sees as the only viable motivation for showing up on time and doing the job—the loyalty of fellow workers to each other.

Mike's ethical sense, honed and developed by his Christian faith, also leads him to suggest to Xers that they have a personal responsibility as well as a contractual obligation to the customers. The customers, he points out, are people too, and serving them is a personal exchange.

Mike finds that his approach works. Xers are motivated when they can see and experience the personal dimensions of the workplace. Mike is a sharp critic of Xer shoddiness, but he has discovered a way to turn it around.

Where Change Is Dangerous

X is now the most racially and ethnically diverse generation in America. It also contains the largest number of immigrants. Tragically, it is the generation with the highest incidence of violence of one toward another. It is the only generation—with the possible exception of the fledgling Millennials now succeeding Xers as youth—that has been well armed and ready to fight it out with Uzis on the streets. The sins of past hatreds and violence have been visited upon this generation. Generation X lives every day in a far more violent world than has any

American generation since the Civil War.

America is now arming itself and sorting itself into hostile camps based on race, class, social status and a variety of other factors. We are rapidly losing the civility and tolerance of one another that make it possible for society to endure. Xers, especially those in the younger half of the generation, are both the principal purveyors and the principal victims of violence.

High-school students in gang-infested schools suffer the brunt of racial divisiveness and violence. Xers still in high school are increasingly being educated in armed camps, and they are desperately searching for workable solutions. Meanwhile, college students operate in a morally segregated and emotionally strained world. Students in these places do make individual and small group forays into the hostile territory of interracial hatred to make friends with people of other races. These are heroic efforts and are often effective.

African-American youth who risk scorn and even violence to befriend whites—and whites who befriend blacks—are at the real cutting edge of social change. They are breaking down walls of hatred by forming personal relationships and moving toward community even though the current wisdom tells them they can't. High-school and college students in growing numbers are beginning to take these risks.

Jeff is an example. As a high-school student, he has seen a friend killed in after-school violence. He has been stopped and robbed at gunpoint and has been threatened any number of times. Yet he continues to try making friends with people in other groups. Refusing to succumb to hatred, he just quietly keeps at it. A leader in his church's youth group, he simply encourages others to follow the teachings of Jesus even when it is difficult to do so.

A twenty-year-old, Bobby, is a member of a racial minority. Also a member of his church community, Bobby has seen more than twenty of his friends die as a result of knife or gunshot wounds. He has been shot himself. At the age of ten he ran away from home and joined a gang because he could no longer tolerate his father's abuse. He never finished high school and is now working part-time and searching for a full-time job—without much hope of finding one.

Bobby lives with friends and has turned away from violence. He helps out his friends when they need lodging or a loan. Survival takes all Bobby's energy. He has contemplated suicide a number of times, but says he won't do it. He finds some hope and help in his church community. He realizes that if he survives long enough this way, he may be able to make some real changes in the future. He believes, "All I can do right now is live one day at a time." Living in the environment he does, Bobby's commitment to nonviolence is heroic.

People like Jeff and Bobby find little help from school systems, public agencies or politicians. They simply adopt a moral and religious position with respect to their violent environment and try to live according to their principles. Without realizing or intending it, they are real agents of social change.

Xers Get a "Bad Rap"

Xers are often criticized on two counts. First, it is said they are "apathetic" because they "don't care" about anything; they are not "altruistic" or "idealistic" as were previous generations—especially Boomers. Second, they are not, it is said, given to much thought about anything. They "just do it."

The truth of the matter is Xers are as altruistic as any generation ever was, but they get no credit for it because they have an aversion to the rhetoric of altruism (here they differ from Boomers). The real but unacknowledged altruism among Xers is not a rerun of the glory days of the sixties, when people of different races linked arms and sang "We shall overcome" as if singing the song would make it so. Xers like Jeff and Bobby who enter this now-dangerous terrain show real commitment, tempered by suffering, shorn of illusions and supported by no rhetoric. They don't talk much about the issues, they "just do it." Xers have little tolerance for the ideological certainties and arrogance of the Boomers and those who define altruism with ideological rather than empirical criteria.

Ideology Versus Real Life

The accusation that Xers are not idealistic is largely a Boomer notion. We must remember that the bitter intergenerational debate between X and Boom is in part an argument about the relationship of language to life. Boomers are as firmly entrenched in their attachment to ideologically pure statement as Xers are to hands-on activity. Xers know from experience that grandiose and monochromatic descriptions of reality are not only inaccurate but downright dangerous.

Boomers in their youth confused the statement of an ideal with its attainment. They still do. "Make love, not war" was and still is a nice sound bite, but it has little meaning as a statement of complex reality. It has no reference to the way the world works. Most Boomers and other elders still don't seem to understand the difference between statement and reality. The endless public debates over "large" issues cause unstifled yawns among Xers, who know they are essentially meaningless. Elders tend to confuse "talking the talk" with "walking the walk." Xers don't.

If one were to set out on a quest for the most tedious group in the American population, one would need search no further than our current crop of ideologues. The right calls for a return to the golden days of patriarchy, a rigid hierarchical reordering of society and the glories of a completely unencumbered free market. These are matched on the left by the totally humorless but equally vapid exponents of absolute political correctness. In the "PC" world, thought and speech are rigorously prescribed and one dare not stray from doctrinaire notions concerning the roles of women, men, minorities and majorities. There is about as much subtlety among the politically correct class as there was in the old Western movies where heroes and villains could be identified by the colors of their hats.

Ideologies would be amusing were they not taken so seriously. The problem is they filter our perceptions into rigid channels, constrict our thinking and thereby limit our options. Current doctrine on the right would return us to the ever-righteous fortress America. On the left it would define female-male relations as fundamentally competitive, and it would banish us into hostile camps of permanently divided races, ethnic groups and social classes. People like Jeff and Bobby are now paying the price for this kind of ideology.

Boomers and other elders seem to adopt a strategy for social change that resembles the World War II battle plans of General Patton in Europe and Admiral Nimitz in the Pacific. They fight their battles head-on—Boomers never saw an ideological battle they didn't like—and are not adverse to taking heavy casualties. Xers, on the other hand, prefer something like the island-hopping strategy adopted by General MacArthur in the southwestern Pacific: Isolate and go around the enemy. Fight only the battles you must, take fewer casualties, and accomplish the objective.

Xer Pragmatism: An Excellent Moral Philosophy

The other part of the bad rap Xers receive is that they "just do it" their way. They are supposedly apathetic with respect to the larger issues of their time and interested only with the practical concerns of life. Not only do they "just do it," but the "it" that they do is limited, partial and tentative with nothing grand and sweeping about it. They have been accused of being "pragmatists." Of course they are—and good for them!

Pragmatism as a formal philosophy is a homegrown American product. It states simply that the truth value of any idea lies in whether it can be verified in practice. The moral and religious value of pragmatism depends on where you begin. Nothing would be more deadly than pragmatism if its starting point were taken to mean that truth is only that which can be discovered in a laboratory and verified by follow-up studies.

Pragmatism is also heinous if the truth one attempts to verify is only "what works for me." But when formulated in a context of real concern for others, from an Xerlike emphasis on the interpersonal and on community, pragmatism may be the only viable antidote to individualism run wild.

During my tour of duty as an army chaplain, I once assisted a soldier to obtain a conscientious-objector discharge from the army on the moral premise of pragmatism. The soldier requested discharge because he would not fight in Vietnam on the moral grounds that war is immoral. War, he argued, has proved—especially in modern times and specifically in Vietnam—that it is unworkable. War achieves no enduring social purpose. It always leads to further violence. War does not work for the good of humanity. It always subverts the common good. Therefore and for that reason, he argued, war violated his conscience and he would not participate in it. The battalion commander disputed his claim: pragmatism, he said, can never provide a viable basis for moral judgments. I argued that in the wider context of the soldier's perspective, pragmatism provided a valid and even superior moral frame of reference. The post commander agreed, and the soldier was discharged.

Searching for simple, limited solutions to the problems of life, Xers operate out of a very sound moral basis—as long as their beginning point, their frame of reference, is "what is good not only for me but also for the community." Xers are realistic pragmatists and generationally humble enough to know they haven't got the answers to the big questions. They are, as we have seen, quietly going to work to make their influence felt—not out of design, but intuitively and even subconsciously.

Pragmatism with respect to political, economic and social systems is essential not only for Xers but for all of us, because it is becoming increasingly clear that no set of systems—anywhere in the world— works very well anymore.

This was brought home to me after the 1992 elections, when a close friend told me that he was in the running for a top-level position in the Clinton administration. I was surprised that he would even let his name be considered, because he had turned down Washington jobs before. He laughed and told me he wouldn't take the position if it was offered, but he liked being considered because it flattered his ego. The reason he would not take any Washington position: "If the plane won't fly, it doesn't make any difference how good the pilot is; it will never get off the ground. And this plane doesn't fly anymore."

Another friend, a highly respected scholar in the fields of sociology and politics, is finishing a book on the political system of a country he knows quite well. I asked him what his next project would be. He replied that he intends to "take a long look" at the failure of political and economic systems worldwide. "Nothing," he says, "works anymore."

That's the point: nothing "flies" or works very well anymore. Generation X, with its hard-headed, nonideological pragmatism suffused with concern for the personal, is working quietly and unobtrusively in the only way that can possibly make things work.

Practical, Limited Solutions: A Religious Vision

Glenn Tinder, political scientist and evangelical Christian, argues in a brilliant book that the gospel really does not permit us to take any political system too seriously.[1] We must, he says, realize that all political systems and the great ideas that undergird them are, by their very nature, always partial and limited. The kingdom of God must not in any way be confused with the various kingdoms of this world. Even societies that seem to be morally better than others are merely political systems.

Xers, by rejecting political grandiosity and embracing what is personal, partial and tentative, are making a collective political statement. They are "downsizing" what we have come to understand as politics. In a world that is moving in two different directions, becoming simultaneously a single global civilization and a collection of millions of disparate small villages, political assumptions that have prevailed for centuries—especially about the sovereignty of the nation-state—are no longer valid.

Politics as practiced in the United States and around the world does not speak to the civilization now evolving. Xers seem to grasp this intuitively. By refusing to pay homage to politics as an ultimately important enterprise, Xers differ significantly from Boomers and from most elders. This refusal to offer sacrifice at political altars is also a subtle and profound religious statement, one not unlike that made in the earliest days of Christianity.

The gospel, as we have seen, locates primary commitments in our personal relationships, first with God and then with our neighbors. From the days immediately after Pentecost, Christians have been a threat to political systems precisely because they refused to bend the knee to the Caesars of this world for whom the political realm was supreme. Only our relationship with God and with our neighbors has Christian significance.

This is not to say that Christians avoid involvement in politics. Quite the contrary: they engage in politics as full-fledged and committed citizens. Politics, after all, has a lot to do with whether interpersonal relationships can take place with justice and fairness. But Christianity does not allow us to find ultimate deliverance through politics or any other human endeavor. With its concentration on the personal dimension and by trying to form community, Generation X is already, as we have indicated previously, "halfway there" not only in its search for meaning and God but also in applying faith to politics.

Tinder makes the point that we are obligated to obey the political authorities but not to take them seriously. Jesus tells us to render to Caesar what is Caesar's, but he never spells out exactly what belongs to Caesar (Matthew 22:21). Paul tells us to obey political rulers out of conscience and not mere expediency because political authority derives from God (Romans 13:1-6). But neither Jesus nor Paul hesitated to act out of conscience in ways that displeased the political authorities. Political authority may, as often as not, pursue paths that are immoral. In such cases the Christian may not follow. One may never invest the political realm with ultimate seriousness. Xers don't.

Interpreting Paul for the present era, Tinder points out that the individual citizen, flawed, limited in perspective and sinful, has no greater wisdom than the political system. For this reason the individual is bound to obey political rulers—unless the laws clearly violate conscience, in which case authority must be resisted. American conservatives, Tinder, argues, tend to take the system too seriously, investing it with wisdom and a quasi-religious *gravitas* it does not possess. Liberals, on the other hand, take *themselves* too seriously, ascribing too much to their individual wisdom and virtue. Xers take neither themselves nor the system seriously. Once again, Generation X, unknowingly perhaps but nonetheless truly, approaches a gospel perspective.

Xers Abroad

Xers are sometimes accused of being people of limited vision, with no interest in what lies beyond their shores. Here again they are compared to Boomers and, in the public mind, suffer by the comparison. But as so often is the case when conventional wisdom is applied to Generation X, the public perceptions are inaccurate.

In their youth, Boomers responded to a call from a young and vibrant president to bear any burden in the cause of freedom. They thronged to the Peace Corps and later to VISTA (Volunteers in Service to America). Exuberant and confident, they marched for civil rights. A bitter war divided the country, and the Boomers were prominent in their opposition. The youthful Boomer impulse was good and generous. It was also very public and boisterous. Xers are no less interested in the world's global needs, nor are they less altruistic, but, as always, they are much quieter about what they are doing.

Generation X has its share of people who commit part of their lives to working among the poor at home or overseas. From our own young adult communities in San Diego we have had our own "peace corps" volunteers, small groups that travel to Mexico to work for the poor.

We have built houses across the border. Ann left us to go to work for VISTA. Bill worked for several months for Habitat for Humanity. These young adults, who are fairly representative of Generation X, have quietly, without adulation or notice, gone off to do their part to make the world a better place.

For some Xers, making the world a better place is as simple as coming to know and care about the people of other lands and cultures. One of the quietest and most unassuming of these generous young adults is John. Growing up as a child of divorce was not easy, nor was his family's constant economic stress. John began his studies at a large public university with one eye always on the cost. He decided on the very difficult premed major because he believed his future lay with medicine. He was fortunate to find a job in a local hospital to help pay for his courses. Exposure on the job to illness, trauma and death only heightened his interest in medicine. Between work and school he still found a little time for dating and fun.

John continued to take his faith and church involvement very seriously. As time went on, he began to realize the social implications of the gospel. How could he, he wondered, be both a Christian and a doctor unless he truly cared about the poor? He began to realize that people in other lands were more seriously afflicted than Americans with poverty, hunger and illness. John decided he must experience firsthand the plight of those less fortunate if he was to be true to both his faith and his chosen profession.

After his third year of undergraduate work, John decided to spend a year in an African country. He would go there to study, to work and to live among the people; then he would complete his premed studies a year behind his class.

When John arrived in Africa, he found himself drawn to the local church that corresponded to his denominational affiliation back home. This church's Sunday-morning worship services included some liturgical dancing. Unlike the few other whites in the congregation, who sat passively and watched the dancing, John decided to take part.

He soon won the admiration of the African congregation. Because he had been an acolyte (one who assists the pastor in celebrating the Eucharist and serving Communion) in his church at home, John asked if he could serve in this capacity in his new African church. The pastor was delighted that he would ask, and soon John was the first Caucasian in more than thirty years to serve this African congregation as an acolyte.

As time went on, John discovered that his African friends from church were becoming true friends—real brothers and sisters. He found that he was hanging out with them, joining in their social activities. He was becoming closer to them than he was to his fellow American students. After several months, John was given a very high honor. He was given an African name at a ceremony held for that purpose.

His time overseas has not been easy. He has suffered illness. When the local police pulled a raid on the university and fired off shots, John was endangered along with his African friends. Common suffering has linked them in a profound way.

As John prepares to return home to complete his undergraduate work and begin medical school, he faces the pain of separation from his dearest friends. And the pain is mutual. Because of the depth of his involvement with his African friends, John's reputation has spread. He is—much to his chagrin, for he is a quiet person—widely known in the region. His friends there will miss him deeply; he has touched many lives. John's letters home to his mother and friends have been published in his parish newsletter, so his experiences are known here as well, and people have been moved by reading them. Whatever John's future may be, there is no doubt that he has already exerted an influence—in Xer style, quietly and by searching for community—on people of two races and two continents.

John and his friends in Africa may never be in positions of power. They may never make the great decisions that have to do with eliminating racial strife and war from an increasingly fractious world. But

John and his African brothers and sisters, members of Global Generation X, are already changing the world in small doses.

Then there is Scott. Scott is a more militant brand of Xer than John. But like John, Scott is Caucasian and shares the same denominational Christian background. At the age of nineteen, he decided that he must face personally the problems of apartheid in South Africa. With help from his church, Scott rounded up the funding to spend some time in South Africa working with the South African Council of Churches. This was during a very bad time in South Africa.

While Scott was attending a church service in Cape Town with his South African black friends, police entered the church, brutally beat the people and hauled many of them off to prison. For his offense of praying publicly with blacks, Scott found himself in the same prison that had housed Nelson Mandela. Upon his release, which was obtained through pressure on the government, Scott returned home to tell the story of a suffering people. He was heard with respect and affection. His story changed minds and touched hearts.

No Complete Solutions

The world is never changed completely. Nothing ever works really well—some things just work better at some times than at others. Civilizations come and go. One world order dies and another takes its place.

Generation X is coming to maturity in time to exert a formative influence at a crucial transition point in history. But sin remains a constant, and the world continues to cry out for redemption and grace.

Redemption and grace are God's gift to the world in the person of Christ, who alone will bring about the world's final change, but who remains in the world in every generation through his body, the Church. We Christians are called to be the Church, acting as agents of change by being "leaven" in the world's cultures and civilizations. To the Church we now turn.

7

THE CHURCH: SETTING THE TABLE FOR GENERATION X

The LORD is my shepherd, I shall not want.
   He makes me lie down in green pastures;
he leads me beside still waters;
   he restores my soul.
He leads me in right paths
   for his name's sake.

Even though I walk through the darkest valley,
   I fear no evil;
for you are with me;
   your rod and your staff—
   they comfort me.

You prepare a table before me
   in the presence of my enemies;
you anoint my head with oil;
   my cup overflows.
Surely goodness and mercy shall follow me
   all the days of my life,
and I shall dwell in the house of the LORD
   my whole life long.
   (Psalm 23)

A Place for Us (Janet)

The world is a hurting place. Our leaders, our shepherds, are often corrupt. Our green pastures are covered with condominiums and disposal sites; our quiet waters are polluted. Our souls are bruised and empty and in great need of restoration. *Right* is a mangled word in today's self-serving society; what used to mean upright, pure and virtuous now means what is right for me. Many of us walk through the valley of death by walking to our cars, going to the cash machine or standing in a post office. We fear evil, and there is little comfort, because we feel alone.

But some of us have found a place where there is solace and comfort, and goodness and love. We were invited into the house of the Lord, and a table was set for us. God was waiting for us. He anointed our heads with oil, and we found that our cups were never empty. Many of us, having experienced the grace of God, have exclaimed as the psalmist did, "I shall dwell in the house of the Lord my whole life long!"

The Church is the place where we find a table set for us. We sit at this table because we are ravenous; we want so much to be fed. And we *are* fed. But quite a bit is required of those who are fed at the Lord's table. He asks that once we are fed, we set a place for someone who has not eaten. And that is the Church. We feed the hungry, and this is a starving world.

It is our job, our joy, our purpose in life to serve others. The Church is where you make it. Whether on the street corner, at school, at home, at work, on the freeway, in the supermarket, at a party or in the post office, it is up to those who have been fed to lead others to the table. It is up to those who have eaten to set a place for those who have not.

Churches today, like doctors today, have become rather specialized. There are Vietnamese churches, the African-American churches, churches for recovering addicts, New Age churches where the Self is God, drive-in churches for the busy and countless other churches that cater to various segments of society. Churches have begun to utilize many of the same marketing techniques used by commercial marketers—and just like commercial marketers, churches tend to target the largest consumer population: the Baby Boomers.

If you watch TV today, you will be hard pressed to find a commercial that does not cater to the Baby Boomer generation. It is a simple matter of marketing to the largest consumer population. Churches have done the same. Churches have laid a table for the generation before us in order to encourage them to return to what they abandoned twenty years ago. They are doing this by investing heavily in child-care and Sunday-school programs, and one church I know of has even expanded its parking lot to fit all the minivans.

The marketing techniques are working. Boomers are returning to the Church. But where are the place settings for Generation X? I am astounded every time I hear someone say that a church does not need a strong high-school or college program because students that age are expected to leave the church and sow their wild oats. These same people expect, as is happening with the Boomers and generations before them, that eventually the Xers will need to give their own children moral guidance and that will bring these wayward souls back to the church. They don't stop to think that the period between high school and childrearing used to be only a couple of years; now ten, fifteen or twenty years may pass between the time a teen sows wild oats and an adult decides to have a family. Meanwhile, an entire generation of people is being ignored by the Church because they do not have children.

I have also heard well-intentioned church leaders say that Generation X is as welcome as any other brand of adult and they see no need for any extra programs to make Xers feel part of the church. Other leaders say they have no young adults in their church, so why set a place for them? And some honestly admit that this generation has a different culture and they haven't the slightest idea how to reach them. What these leaders do not understand is how Generation X perceives the Church.

Generation X sees the Church as an institution like all others, and Generation X does not trust institutions. Since our birth we have witnessed the Watergate scandal, the Iran-contra scandal, the BCCI scandal and the moral scandals of politicians and judges. We have seen local and national governments from Haiti to Japan crumble because of corruption. Even Hollywood has lost much of its glamour as we have watched beautiful, talented people suffer from overdose and overkill. Many of our athletic heroes have become irresponsible millionaires with dwindling respect for the games we pay them so well to play.

When Xers think of religion, they think of Jim and Tammy Faye Bakker. They think of extravagant televangelists bilking money from old women on social security. They think of Catholic priests abusing small children, and they think of the extreme political right wing that denounces much of what we call freedom. Xers, on the whole, regard religious institutions as they do all other institutions—as not to be trusted.

But we are still searching for God. We are still trying to fill the God space, and we are continuously on the run from a dispassionate and fearful world. We are looking for a place to rest, someone we can trust. We are looking for a community, and like all people before us, we want to be part of something bigger than ourselves. We want lines drawn for moral guidance. We want living examples of purity, honesty and love. We want a family that will love us unconditionally, and we want to believe in something.

So how does the Church reach this generation? The Church embodies community and offers a place to belong. Beside the worship liturgy itself, it is community that will draw Generation X to the church and to the altar of God. Christians can offer hope by offering a community based on God's love for his people and the people's love for each other.

It is really rather simple. An entire generation of people lack affection because of broken homes, feel disposable because of technology and see little hope in conventional methods of creating change. The Christian community can offer the open arms of a loving God, the body of Christ in which each part is as vital as another, and God's justice—fearful, true and merciful.

Whose Table Is It? (Bill)

Janet believes that the churches have targeted Boomers in a variety of ways but have failed to provide place settings at the Lord's table for Xers. I believe she is correct—though there are some outstanding exceptions—but the problem runs even deeper than that.

During the turbulent sixties, church leadership was composed of people who should have been—but were not—wiser than the adolescent Boomers. The failure of the Church at this time was its inability to distinguish the real moral and religious turmoil that engulfed the nation from the massive adolescent rebellion that occurred at the same time. During the sixties the Church lost large numbers of its young people. Now it is trying to get them back as middle-aged forty-somethings—so the Church is, as Janet says, "targeting" the Boomers. Church leadership now, of course, includes Boomers—but not Xers, who are still too young.

Adolescence is always a time of rebellion and self-absorption, but in most historical eras elders have provided the young with the kind of guidance that allows them to grow into mature adults. Leaders in the Church have traditionally understood this. In the sixties, however, the leadership of the American Church reverted to the kind of theological and moral shallowness that is a hallmark of adolescence. Boomers went off "in search of themselves" on the grand historical stage of the time, and their elders, in adolescent fashion, went with them in the name of "relevance."

Without realizing it, both evangelical and mainline wings of the Church adopted a Boomer ethos—as did much of America. As the mainline churches drifted in the direction of syncretism and psychologizing or watering down the gospel, many evangelicals moved toward a narrow, uncritical and quite unbiblical fundamentalism. Evangelicals and mainline churches mistakenly "split the difference" between them.

The mainline drift carried the potential to submerge the gospel in the secular culture, while the evangelicals tended to identify the gospel with the more virulent militaristic and individualistic forms of American civil religion. Each of these proclivities stressed the importance of the individual self rather than the common good. The quest for the self or "the voyage to the interior" became normative.

The American Church thus adopted Boomer-type self-absorption. American Christianity has come to resemble a large shopping mall in which the individual can meet his or her "religious needs." In all American religious communities, even among Roman Catholics and evangelicals, there has been a "therapeutic thinning out of belief and practice, a withdrawal into the narrow boundaries of religious community itself, or both."[1]

Both evangelicals and mainline Christians, in very different ways, inhabit a highly individualistic religious domain in their efforts to address the rapidly shifting culture. Thus they adopt what is fundamentally a Boomer focal point. This is the wider sense in which the Church has set a table for Boomers. Xers are right in pointing to the failures of the Church in their regard, but the Church first failed the Boomers by setting a table with the junk food that adolescents so dearly love but that contains no real sustenance.

The Church's table must be set again with much richer fare if it is to nourish Generation X. But Christian Xers are already at work preparing that table, providing it with food that is both wholesome and savory. Paradoxically, the dishes they bring to it may prove appealing as well to middle-aged Boomers who, after decades of junk food, are now close to spiritual starvation.

The Church for Xers: A Variety of Voices

"The Church," Ben, a Lutheran, believes, "is the family that we were supposed to have, but most of us never had. It's different from the rest of the world." He notes that in the Church "everybody is present at the supper table, unlike most families today. And there's no absentee Father."

For Ann, an Episcopalian, the Church is "the place where we can be completely ourselves and try to love each other with the unconditional love of Christ." In the Church, Ann says, "we all bring our imperfections. There you can be openly imperfect instead of trying to act within the boundaries of a rigid society." Ann believes also that "once we have come together as hurting people, we must get into a highly social mode and go out to others." She is convinced that a Christian community must never become a clique.

Kristie, a Presbyterian, sees the Church as "a place of believers and a place of worship." But for her it is also "my major support system, a neat place to feel free to celebrate God." She finds in the Church "a sense of the Holy Spirit and a place to learn to live like Christ— and to relate to each other in Christ."

Vladimir, an Eastern Rite Roman Catholic, sees the Church as "a shelter or house of love. Christ is standing within it with his arms outstretched, saying, 'Come to me, all you who labor and are heavily burdened, and I will refresh you.' "

For Elva, an Episcopalian, the Church is "the place where we bear each other's burdens and Christ bears them all for us." Elva also believes that the Church hears Jesus saying, "My burden is sweet and my yoke is light."

Ben, Ann, Kristie, Vladimir and Elva, all in their twenties, are members of our San Diego young adult community. Xers from other churches and fellowships have similar insights.

John, a member of InterVarsity Christian Fellowship and a Baptist, sees the Church as a " 'space station' where you come in, are supported and go out again." Richard, a member of a Baptist campus fellowship, sees the Church as the "embodiment of believers; it is a total haven from the ills of society." His friend Brad, also a Baptist, sees the Church as a place to "praise God and be open to him." In the Church "there is no need to be lonesome."

Cuong, a member of a Roman Catholic campus community, sees the Church as "home, a nurturing place, a shelter, a hideout from the daily mess." But it is also for him "a place of service where I can use my talents and skills." (He is a music leader within his community.) His friend Nancy, a Methodist, says, "I find God in my friends."

Scott, an InterVarsity leader and a Baptist, delights in the "variety within the Church, because there is a place for everyone." The first thing about the Church in his experience is that "I am accepted."

Carl, a member of an Eastern Orthodox campus fellowship, finds that for him the Church is "a communion of love that includes all the saints, living and dead." Carl finds the Church exemplified best in worship, where "we gather together and sometimes we seem to ascend to Christ, though Christ is already there."

Though there is a great variety in the understanding of the Church for these Xers, there is clearly a prevalent theme conveyed by the imagery they use. The Church is refuge, a home of love, a haven, hideout, support system, space station, place where I am not lonesome, place where I am accepted. The Church is a supper table where all are welcome. The Church is a place where Jesus stands with outstretched arms, taking upon himself our burdens. The Church for them is also the place where we must set the table for others, where we too stand with outstretched arms, welcoming others who are similarly burdened.

The Church as a Haven

These young adults are saying essentially the same things I have been hearing from Xers since the late 1980s. Earlier in the book I mentioned a student retreat during which Xers unburdened themselves of overwhelming stresses and anxieties. The group followed through shortly afterward with a Bible study on Paul's "bear one another's burdens," and that night a similar outpouring took place. As a result of these sessions, I asked the young adult community to design a model of the Church that they would find most meaningful and appropriate to them. They came up with "The Church as Stress Haven."

Essentially what they envisioned was a church community of young adults in which people would come and simply be themselves, sharing their burdens, sinfulness, weakness and fragility in the context of the unconditional love of Christ. This was a marvelous and beautiful notion, but at first I was bothered by the primacy given to the Christian community as a place of refuge, retreat, haven. I thought the primary emphasis should have been on the Church's mission to evangelize and serve the world. When I made this point, the community argued that while these missions are essential, the Church must *first* be a haven and refuge *before* it can work effectively in the world.

I have come to realize that they are right. I believe that most Christians older than Generation X—including Boomers—do not realize that the Xer experience of life and the Church is fundamentally different from theirs. I am now convinced that Xer priorities with respect to the Church are more appropriate to the age in which we live than are mine. The Church must still be the servant Church, but it must *first* be a haven. I have adopted an Xer paradigm: the Church as oasis.

The Church as Oasis in the Desert

In all things Generation X seeks community, that essential antidote to its youthful estrangements. The search for meaning and God, the complicated quest for personhood, the ways in which it goes about building a different world order: all acquire their defining features from an unslakable thirst for that which is communitarian and highly interpersonal.

X became "a generation alone" because it was—and still is—left to sink or swim on its own, strangely isolated from its elders in a most uncongenial world. The alienation and abandonment we described earlier confront Xers with a fundamental choice between cynicism/ nihilism and a buoyancy of soul that springs from personal relationships. It is a choice thrust upon them by the severity of their surroundings.

Happily, Xer aloneness imparts the momentum for a generational pilgrimage in the direction of community. Those who wander through a desert are always looking for a genuine oasis. As we have seen, members of Generation X encounter mirages along their journey, but they have discovered that community offers real water to the parched soul along with rest and refuge to the weary traveler.

But not all oases have abundant moisture, nor are all havens equally secure. The desert through which Xers travel is so dry and hostile that their place of refuge must be lavish in its water and very well protected against the "whirlwind of barbarism" that blows off the desert.

We know of only one such sanctuary, and it is blessed with limitless resources. It is a garden that intrudes upon the desert. The One who tends it quenches our thirst, protects us from harm and brings us into community with each other and with himself.

Designed originally to dwell in the garden, we wander nonetheless in the desert. But the Gardener, our Designer, has promised to transform the desert into a final and lasting garden that we shall inhabit eternally. And in the meantime, between now and eternity, an oasis is always available—the Church.

The Church at the Cutting Edge

Christian Xers, having been called to the community of faith, have discovered the ultimate remedy for the pain that afflicts their generation, for they journey—together and in community—with the One who banishes all despair and leads us into hope. The Christians of Generation X thus stand out in starker contrast on their social horizon than have young Christians of previous generations. My own generation, for example, had no experience as an age cohort of the kind of nihilism that afflicts the young today. For us the Church was a community of hope in a world that also held out to us great promise and hope.

A community of hope is what the Church must be to Generation X. But as Janet points out, most Xers view the Church as just another institution that is not to be trusted. Karen, a member of a Baptist fellowship, agrees. She notes that though she and many other Christian Xers find the Church to be a haven, her non-Christian contemporaries are suspicious of all institutions and tend to be cynical about any claims the Church might make for itself.

Karen believes this contrast defines the missionary venture of the Church to her generation. By being in demonstrable fact a haven—in ways Xers can experience firsthand—the Church evangelizes among Generation X. The "Haven Church" establishes the pattern for how the Church will serve the world. It provides as well a paradigm for the postmodern world: create a haven for everyone and invite them to come. This Church model is simple, clear, direct and deep. It removes the disjuncture between what the Christian does in church and in the world, for in both church and world you create a place of refuge and invite people into it. Janet's metaphor is on target: the Lord has set a table for us, and we now go and invite others to the table.

The Church can be considered under any of the metaphors we have used—haven, oasis, a set table—only because of its essential connection with God through Jesus Christ. As we mentioned earlier, God "got physical" with us in Jesus. This is stated quite literally in Scripture: "The Word was with God, and the Word was God . . . and the Word became flesh and 'pitched his tent' among us" (John 1:1, 14 literally rendered). And again: "Christ Jesus . . . though he was in the form of God, did not regard equality with God as something to be exploited, but emptied himself, taking the form of a slave, being born in human likeness" (Philippians 2:5-7). Christians refer to this as the *incarnation* (enfleshment) of God within humanity. God remains physical with us through the body of Christ, the Church. Another physical image: Christ is the "vine," we are the "branches" (John 15:5).

The task of the Church in every time and place is to become physically rooted or planted in the culture. The Church as it emerges within Generation X has an enormous assignment: planting itself with deep roots in postmodern civilization. The contrast between the emerging Xer church and the current church is significant because, I believe, the older model deals with a world that is dying while the

Xer cutting edge addresses a world that is coming to be.

Being the Church at the cutting edge is very difficult. I learned this many years ago in the Japanese mission. A remarkable old German missionary who had spent many years in Japan spoke one day about the perplexing problem of preaching the gospel and planting the Church in the Japanese culture, which remains largely impervious to Christianity. I can remember his words almost verbatim after almost thirty years: "The real question is not how to preach the gospel to the Japanese in their own culture, because Japanese society is being changed by the emergence of a worldwide technological civilization. This will change not only the Japanese but all cultures. The real question is, How do you preach the gospel to a technological civilization?"

The tendencies we see arising among the Christians of Generation X are enormously important, because they represent an intuitive and practical effort to live as Christians in this technological civilization. This is a pioneering venture that is likely to shape the future. The shape of the future is already visible through a few "snapshots" of the Xer Church.

The "Galatians Church" of Generation X

"Bear one another's burdens, and in this way you will fulfill the law of Christ" (Galatians 6:2).

The Church as it comes into being for Generation X takes on, as it must, the generational characteristics and aspirations of young adults. We have described these throughout the book. The generation alone, always in search of community, becomes community in the fullest sense when its Christian members gather as church. These young adult groups, at least the ones Janet and I observe and in which we participate, are, quite literally, oases in a spiritual desert.

The delightful thing about Xers is that they "just do it." They really do make the Church into a place of refuge, an oasis in the desert. They truly do invite others to share this oasis with them. The Xer experience of Church as refuge is extraordinarily powerful, not only for young adults but also for those of us older folk who are privileged to join them.

These young Christians, isolated in their faith from large numbers of their contemporaries—in ways my generation was not—come together for prayer, Bible study, worship services, sharing or just plain fun, and they offer each other spiritual support at a depth my generation did not in an era that was more congenial to youth. Xers truly become a church community in which the biblical Church is clearly and impressively identifiable.

One Body, One Faith, One Baptism

But what is this Church we've been talking about? It is a broken and wounded group of people with a scarred, turbulent history. Yet Paul tells us clearly that it is one single body of believers. "There is one body and one Spirit, just as you were called to the one hope of your calling, one Lord, one faith, one baptism, one God and Father of all, who is above all and through all and in all" (Ephesians 4:4-6).

Tragically, we Christians have paid little heed to Paul's description. For centuries the Church has been openly split into branches that have institutionalized their separateness and have acted toward each other in a most unchristian fashion. The division of the Church into Catholic, Protestant and Eastern Orthodox warring factions has been a scandal.

During the second half of the twentieth century, the branches of the Church have drifted closer to each other because of the growing understanding that we share a common faith in Christ. And Xers' generational inclinations toward unity and cohesiveness strongly incline them to reject denominational hostility and to accept Paul's great vision for the Church. Young adult believers most often identify themselves as "Christian" rather than as members of a particular denomination.

Xers seem to know intuitively that the Church is not Protestant or

Catholic or Orthodox. It is all three: Protestant *and* Catholic *and* Orthodox. It is, as Christian Xers know in their bones, the one Church described by Paul, the only Church adequate to the postmodern world.

One of the richest words in the New Testament is *koinōnia,* which translates as "fellowship" or "sharing"—no English equivalent catches the full meaning of this magnificent word. We are called into *koinōnia* with each other and with God. "Participants" in the divine nature in 2 Peter 1:4, "sharing" in the body and blood of Christ in 1 Corinthians 10:16, and "fellowship" among Christians in Acts 2:42 all come from the same root. *Koinōnia* is the source of our unity.

In this book we have referred to the Church (with a capital *C*) to describe this great *koinōnia* reality. When we use the word *Church,* we mean the one described by Paul. This is the Church that exists in response to the prayer of Jesus "that they may all be one. As you, Father, are in me and I am in you, may they also be in us" (John 17:21). This is the Great Church to which all Christians belong.

When we say *church* (with a small *c*) we mean local churches, parish congregations, small Bible study groups and fellowships. These different churches are all part of the Church, which is found "wherever two or three are gathered in my name." The Church is found in each denomination and in each single gathering of believers, which reflects in turn the Great Church, the magnificent *koinōnia.*

As Paul tells us, the body is very diverse, having many members and many gifts. The rich diversity found historically across the Christian spectrum, within Protestantism, Roman Catholicism and Eastern Orthodoxy, belongs to all of us as a common heritage. This beautifully diverse Church with a common faith is the one that is arising within the heart of Generation X. It is the Church in its fullest sense.

Being in Christ

"There is no longer slave or free, there is no longer male and female; for all of you are one in Christ Jesus" (Galatians 3:28).

The Xers' preliminary sketch of the Church takes another cue from Paul's letter to the Galatians. The Spirit seems to be leading them in a way that coincides with their generational propensities. Always in search of community, these young adults are more willing than their elders to take seriously Paul's "neither-nor" passage. They want to break down the barriers that separate one group of people from another.

Though their elders might still struggle with it, Xers have largely and in principle resolved the male-female distinctions in the Church.[2] Having experienced the powerful leadership and influential presence of dynamic young women in campus fellowships and young adult communities—and in many of their churches—Christian Xers do not deny the full spiritual equality of women with men. This is simply no longer an issue for Xers. All leadership positions within the Church of Generation X will be open equally to women and men. This will ultimately include the Roman Catholic Church and those Protestant churches that now resist the trend.

And X is the most racially mixed generation in American history. It seeks community of the kind that breaks down racial barriers. InterVarsity Christian Fellowship and other Christian ministries that have traditionally been largely Caucasian are now trying to foster racial inclusiveness. Though Christians of different races often form their own fellowships, they are growing more willing to view other groups of different races as fully their brothers and sisters in Christ. On campuses we see this tendency especially as we come together for public celebrations of our common faith. This flies in the face of the racial and ethnic isolation that is so prevalent on campuses today—it is another instance of the Church's acting over and against prevailing cultural norms.

Today Paul might add to his proclamation: "There is neither a leadership elite nor a follower class." The Church of Generation X will have less hierarchical and bureaucratic structure. A generation that distrusts large institutions but seeks communities of real sharing is already in the process of "relativizing" and using pragmatically the institutional machinery of churches and fellowships. *Does it do the job?* That's the question Xers ask inside as well as outside the Church. If it no longer delivers the goods, then a church structure that's been around since the "the day after the Reformation" will go when Xers get their hands on it.

This applies to the role of clergy as well. The Church has always had ordained leadership and always will. But the relationship of ordained leadership to the entire community has differed greatly in different periods of history, among the different branches of the Church and from place to place within the same denomination.

The Reformation accentuated the "priesthood of all believers" in contradistinction to the Roman Catholic emphasis on the hierarchical priesthood. Protestantism, however, never developed the full potential contained in its original impulse in this direction. Clergy in all churches are still clearly delineated from laity. Xers will narrow the gap.

Until now, clergy, because of their theological training and institutional position, have been considered to be the principal spiritual leaders and guides of the Church. They preached the gospel from the pulpit, interpreted it for their hearers and sent the congregation out into the world to live according to it. Laity were not usually considered equals of the clergy as spiritual leaders.

Xers are different. They do not wait for the blessing of their elders or of authority in secular life. Nor do they wait for the clergy in the Church. They are quite egalitarian and democratic with respect to their exercise of all the spiritual gifts. They are not afraid to hold one another accountable, to teach, to lead in prayer and to offer real spiritual friendship and direction to each other—and to their elders. Young adults who become clergy will doubtless reject the older model in favor of a more egalitarian Xer one.

There has always been in the Church a significant group that counterbalanced the leadership of clergy. Xers of all denominations are to be found firmly within this group. Not only have they inherited the tradition, they have revived it.

The early desert hermits, male and female, who exerted enormous influence over the Church in the early centuries were mostly unordained. Monasticism, which followed the desert hermits, was largely a lay movement. Monks and nuns traditionally took Church authority quite lightly. Benedict, the founder of Western monasticism, refused to be ordained a priest. Down through the centuries in both Western and Eastern Catholicism, through the Reformation and including both Protestant and Catholic branches of the Church, there has always been a tradition of great lay spiritual leaders. These have been among the most marvelous spiritual guides the Church has ever had. Some ordained clergy, hermits and monks themselves, have sided with and endorsed this movement of the laity.

Many Christians of Generation X seem to fall within this tradition in which lay leadership arises, is recognized and is given full rein. There is no overt challenge to clergy, no disrespect and certainly no Boomer-type nonsense like "don't trust anyone over thirty." The new leaders stand alongside the clergy as spiritual equals and friends, not as a sociologically distinct group.

Until He Comes

"For as often as you eat this bread and drink the cup, you proclaim the Lord's death until he comes" (1 Corinthians 11:26).

Charles M. Olsen once described "the Three-Legged Stool of Prayer."[3] With four, five or even ten legs a stool can stand, but you cannot stand a stool on fewer than three legs. The Christian life, Olsen contends, stands on three necessary legs. The first is individual prayer—of which we will have more to say in the final chapter.

The second is the small group of prayer, support and study. Our small "Galatians Groups" provide our community with this leg of the stool. Most young adult communities engage in weekly Bible study and prayer, and ours is no exception. We also have discussed theological issues, faith and modern philosophy, creation and evolution. We have shared our brokenness and our hopes and dreams. All this is common and quite standard for Xer Christian communities. Participation in such groups is a good way to understand the Church as it is being shaped by Generation X. Small group fellowships are always a window into the life of a church, for small groups are necessary for the spiritual health of any religious community. Xers are gathering in great numbers in these groups.

The third leg of the stool of prayer is the larger formal Sunday worship, wherein the individual and the smaller groups are taken into the skeletal structure of the body of Christ. The individual and small group concerns enter publicly, with the entire community present, into the great act of redemption that took place on the cross and was shown to be complete at the empty tomb.

The Church is fully itself when it assembles to worship its Lord. In our own young adult community, we gather regularly for Sunday worship each in our own parishes—as do all Christians everywhere and always. We also gather together once a month to celebrate the Eucharist in what we have come to call "Creative Worship."

These Creative Worship services differ from Sunday-morning worship in several ways that demonstrate the Xer influence even on the more formalized eucharistic worship of the Church. Though the services are sponsored by Episcopalian and Lutheran campus ministries, we attract evangelicals, Roman Catholics, mainline Christians and others from across the Christian spectrum.

The participants have devised ways to include the richness of the various traditions represented. Prayer is spontaneous and free. Prayer leaders are always Xers, never the clergy. Music is most often contemporary—and sometimes written for the occasion—though we also use traditional hymns and folk music. The music of Taizé, the Protestant-originated though now ecumenical religious community in France, has influenced us greatly. It is prayerful and leads to silence and contemplation.

Scripture readings are selected to emphasize a theme—unlike the Sunday-morning worship, which always follows a set three-year cycle of readings. Though one of the clergy preaches a short homily, there is always a longer period of shared reflection on the passages. Some of the most remarkable "sermons" I have ever heard have come from these shared reflections. I never fail to learn something about the gospel from listening to Xers articulate its meaning within the very heart of the worship service.

Instead of taking up a monetary collection, we invite anyone who has written a song or a poem to offer it to the community. Thus we have heard Jane sing a folk song she wrote about seeing the face of Jesus in her homeless schizophrenic brother. We have heard a love letter to her husband by a young woman who had just learned she was pregnant. We have heard Tracey's songs and poems. We have heard reflections on what it means to live in a wheelchair, and we have been treated to beautiful poetry by those who had come close to despair. We have also heard songs that sparked delight and laughter.

In this small assembly the entire Church is present in all its beauty. The panoply of human gifts is offered to God—as are the individual selves of those who offer. We are conscious that these gifts are then offered to the Father in the eucharistic prayer—the great and ancient prayer of the Church, which is also contemporary and flexible. We are given in return a share in the bread and the cup and thus "proclaim the Lord's death until he comes." But the One who has died is now risen, and so we are united—in all our individuality and uniqueness, in our moments of joy and sorrow—in the death and resurrection of the Lord.

This third leg on our community stool of prayer, that moment when we "proclaim the Lord's death" in the Eucharist, has become extraordinarily powerful and precious to us. These Creative Worship services have given me what I believe is a glimpse into the future of the Church that Generation X will someday lead. If the spiritual depth, power and creativity of these young adults engaged in the formal public and eucharistic worship of God gives any indication of what the Church will be like in the future, then the Church will be in very good hands, for the Xer carpenters are already at work, refurbishing and freshening up all three legs of the ancient stool.

Set Free for Freedom

At a recent Bible study, the young adult community was considering Galatians once again. This time we began with chapter 5. One of the few "old-timers" in the group remembered the study two years before on bearing one another's burdens—the study that had opened the floodgates of problems. Someone else remarked that the burdens are still there, but somehow it is different. We are not mired down in them. They are still there, but we are free. For Christ has set us free.

These Xers are still immersed in the same hostile culture, still struggling with the issues we have discussed in this book. They are seeking and finding community. They are attempting to change at least a small portion of the world. But for them, the bottom line is quite simply that we are not condemned to fear, to pessimism, to nihilism. Their hearts can climb toward God, they can sing and truly rejoice. This is the gift they have received from Christ—the freedom to be free, not to be weighed down, not to be oppressed and heavy of soul, for the human spirit was created to ascend to God.

As I watched their spirits soar, I realized that Generation X has within its ranks Christians of great stature. I knew that the Xers in this "Galatians Group" had been delivered from their generational bondage. In that moment I too understood the passage in a new way, for they had shown me that it is indeed for this kind of freedom that Christ has set us free.

8

TAKE IT ALL: RADICAL CHRISTIANITY

The Surrender (Janet)

I was driving north on Interstate 5 when I told God, "Take it all." I had been trying since I knew how to maintain control over every aspect of my life, including that ever-changing God space. I had been told over and over to "give your life to God." That was supposed to make everything better. Well, it did and it didn't.

I thought I had surrendered my life to God years before that drive up I-5, but that day I realized that I had only surrendered the parts I did not like about myself, with the hope that they would be changed for the better. So what I did that day was surrender as well everything I *liked*, everything I found useful, imaginative, creative or excellent about myself and my surroundings. I told God that I was working for him from then on, and that I had these things to offer.

There was an immediate sense of affirmation. I felt as though I had come home to welcoming arms: "We have been waiting for you." It felt good; it was beautifully safe.

But that was the last day for quite some time that I felt so good. For I had finally opened a door that led down a long path toward God. I saw immediately that this path is very well lit, and it hurt me to look into it, because I was more accustomed to the darker path I had chosen to walk.

The first few weeks after making that decision were terribly difficult for me. I no longer felt the warmth; in fact, I could no longer feel God's presence at all. I could not understand why at the very moment I surrendered to him he would walk away. What I realize now is that I was being beckoned to follow, and following God can be painful.

Goodness was as a light, and the closer I came to that light the more it exposed some very dark corners. At every turn this light would expose some dark, dusty, cobwebbed corner of my life, and I would be forced to examine it and clean it out. The light was relentless in its search, and I felt very dirty and very ugly inside. It took weeks for God to complete that initial search into the corners of my being, and it took even longer for me to attend to each part of my being that required change, repentance or nurturing. But as time wore on, I gained a very real sense of purpose and value.

It has since been explained to me that the feeling of abandonment from God has, from ancient times, been described as the Cloud of Unknowing. I knew somehow that God was there, but I could not see or feel him. I was simply feeling beckoned, and I followed. Nothing in my short life has ever been more rewarding.

I am not alone in my experiences. I continue to encounter people of all ages along this path that leads toward God, but more and more I am finding that people my age, the people of Generation X, are choosing to walk down this path. They are realizing, in great numbers, that our world is lacking meaning because it is lacking spirituality. Only God can put meaning into a meaningless world.

Those of us who have allowed God to clean out and inhabit our God space have been made to feel valuable and clean. We have been transformed. The houses of our hearts have been cleaned and organized, and we are no longer ashamed to let anyone in. Instead we open the door of our heart and invite others in, and through others we find meaning and joy. This is where we begin to change the world.

Going to the Root (Bill)

What happened between God and Janet on I-5 is not uncommon among Christians who take their faith seriously. Though this kind of surrender to God was at one time thought to be limited to people with a good deal of wisdom and life experience, it is becoming increasingly common in Generation X. I know many young adults, including people still in their teens, who have similarly turned their lives over to God. This is a crucial step along the way to a radical following of Jesus Christ—remember, *radical* really means "pertaining to the root or origin." It means also something "fundamental" that sets a person or thing apart, as in "radical difference."[1]

Telling God to "take it all" brings a person to the root and origin of all being, including one's own existence. It is an acknowledgment that all of the self belongs to God, with nothing left over. Such a surrender to God, with the intent to hold nothing back, differs in a most radical way from the self-centered impulses of our culture.

This radical step is supremely important for Xers in search of wholeness, hope, meaning, community and happiness in a predatory world. Real hope and truly grounded happiness are inaccessible until the "God space" is filled. This is because the soul left to its own devices is largely empty, except for yearnings and tendencies that impel it toward the perfect satisfaction that only God can give.

We have already reported the inclination to friendship and community we find among Xers—which is remarkable, given their enculturation into a society ruled by the Imperial Self. Now we are exploring something even more exceptional—a willingness on the part of a small but significant part of a generation, raised in the most secular, amoral environment in Western history, to commit themselves totally to God. More and more Xers seem to be taking this step, but they are also discovering, as did Janet, the ancient and biblical truth that friendship with God always entails a struggle.

The real question from the dominant perspective in our secularized, consumerized society is, Why should there be any relationship with God at all, to say nothing of a struggle and subsequent surrender of self to God? Why indeed should a generation of supposed young cynics and pragmatists who have very little trust in any institutions—including those of religion—be willing to surrender to a God they can't see and can't measure? Janet once articulated an Xer perspective when she exclaimed with great passion: "Xers have steel-coated souls. The self is all we have! Why should we give it to God?"

The answer to this question is quite simple—an answer Janet and countless others know very well from their own experience: they tell God to "take it all" because God is calling them directly and by name into this kind of personal relationship with himself.

We often speak of the Christian as "having a personal relationship with Jesus." But we have forgotten in modern centuries, especially in the affluent United States, that having a personal relationship with Jesus is depicted in Scripture as being rather difficult because it means following him all the way to the cross.

In the earliest Christian centuries people were tortured and killed because they followed Jesus. During some periods of history people went out into the deserts of North Africa and the Middle East to live as hermits and into monasteries so that they might have a closer personal relationship with Jesus. Xer Christians, because they live in a spiritual wasteland, seem to have something of the spirit of those ancient Christians who suffered much for the sake of Jesus. Xer Christians stand in starker contrast to the secular society, to their elders and even to the mores of their own peers than did earlier generations of American Christians. Thus they endure more for the sake of Jesus at a young age than did their elders. They have to be radical Christians.

A woman much older and wiser than I—a Roman Catholic nun— was talking not long ago about the growing number of people who seem to be coming to this type of radical relationship with God. She said, "The Spirit is moving across a society in despair." She is convinced that radical Christians serve a great function in society: "They hold up mirrors to a blind world."

She is absolutely right, and her statement especially defines the task of the teenage and twentysomething Christians whose lives and careers are just beginning. As the world becomes blinder by the day, the mirror young Christians hold up must be clearer and brighter than the dull and tarnished glass we elders have occasionally raised above the crowd.

The Christians of Generation X must be a gutsy, hardy bunch, willing to take risks—even the risk of following Jesus to the cross. They've got to be radical enough to tell God to take everything and persistent enough to accept the consequences of that commitment. The good news is, that's just the kind of people God is raising up within Generation X.

The Paradoxical Presence of God

Let's look at Janet's experience—which is not all that unusual among Christian Xers—as a model by which to understand how the radical following of Jesus takes root in the soul. Janet first struggled with God over how much of herself she would really offer to him. She thought she had already given everything over to God by surrendering the broken parts of herself to be "fixed." God let her know, in ways she resisted at first, that what she had already given was really not enough—she was being called to offer her whole self to him. Having grappled with God, she finally gave in. Initial struggle and final surrender to God are biblical themes that are relevant to people's experience of God in every generation.

Janet's sense of affirmation, of feeling safe, when she had finally committed herself to God is also a very common experience, one that seems to be crucial—and is often more prolonged than it was in her case. This is the most pleasing aspect of the Christian life of faith—

it certainly is for me and for most people I know. It corresponds to the initial reactions of the disciples when Jesus began his ministry and they were entranced by his presence. Many people expect to bask in this kind of religious glow throughout their lives—but that seldom happens, because God has something else in mind.

The next element in Janet's experience is more troubling—the sense of God's support and affirmation vanishes. Why? When, after some struggle, one has finally told God to "take it all" and then been affirmed in this commitment, why does God recede, strangely hiding himself within a kind of "cloud," and allow one to feel almost abandoned? Why does a commitment to give one's life to God often result not in a heightened exuberance but in a sense of spiritual desolation? Why is following Christ painful?

As we shall see, this relates to Jesus' insistence that his followers walk with him on the way to the cross. Exploring this dimension of the Christian experience places us at the foot of the cross with Jesus—and like the original disciples, we do not find Golgotha a congenial place.

The next element Janet describes is feeling ugly and dirty as the light of goodness exposes some dark, dusty, cobwebbed corners of the self. This again is a classic Christian experience. It is connected with repentance and healing and accepting God's offer of new life in Christ.

Janet offered herself in service to God—she was going to work for him—but then she, and many other Xers, had to walk away from a society that is largely without spirituality. Finally, she was ready to reenter society and change it by opening the doors of her heart, now cleaned and transformed, and inviting others in. This offering of self to God defines both the nature of Christian service and the way Xers will work to change the world. It also resonates with the biblical injunction to be in the world but not of it.

There is a powerful set of paradoxes at the heart of Janet's "take it all" experience: the relentless power of light in darkness, the discovery of meaning and purpose without discernible reason, the sense of being beckoned by a presence she could no longer feel. All of this relates to the shattering, unexpected, overpowering experience that remains the cornerstone of our faith—the resurrection of Jesus.

Why There Is a Struggle

The psalmist speaks for all of us—at least at some time in our lives—with the cry: "My soul is full of troubles, and my life draws near to Sheol. . . . You have put me in the depths of the Pit, in the regions dark and deep" (Psalm 88:3, 6). With this lament the psalmist spoke to a universal condition—his words are a cry of the heart from the very depths of the human condition.

Ordinarily this kind of lament is heard from people who have lived long enough to realize through experience that many youthful dreams will not be fulfilled, that physical health inevitably fails and that faith in God does not preclude pain, even tragedy. As someone remarked: "Life always ends badly—in death." To cry out with the psalmist from "the depths of the Pit, in the regions dark and deep" is simply to be human.

Many people feel the approach of spiritual desolation in their lives, and these days, young adults in unprecedented numbers are among them. But much of modern Western Christianity—and certainly the American version—attempts to fend off this winter of the soul. People seek instead the "warm fuzzies" our culture has come to identify with religious faith. "Happy face" religion and "have a nice day" spirituality are pervasive in our culture, even though, from a Christian perspective, these are expressions of spiritual adolescence. People who cling to these religious toys not only are forced—in the name of what they think is faith—to deny their true feelings but are destined to remain spiritual adolescents all their lives.

I have repeated several times Janet's comment that Xers are "halfway to the gospel." Nowhere is this more true than in the extent to which large numbers of Xers are able to identify with the cry of the psalmist. As we have already explained, X differs significantly from previous American generations because its members came of age as the American dream was collapsing, and the expectations of the modern world along with it. The world was not what they'd been told it would be. They had bought into something that turned out to be bogus. This is a major source of spiritual desolation. Paradoxically, Generation X has reached sufficient spiritual maturity to have the affinity for the psalmist that eludes many of their supposedly more mature elders.

Spiritual desolation can come about for several reasons. For a great many Xers it arises, as we have said, merely from the context of their lives or their generational experience. For these people the spiritual cloud is simply there and has no discernible purpose. Their primary and lifelong task is to find the meaning of their emptiness and discover a way to fill the void. Radical Christianity provides just such a path.

Spiritual bleakness also comes about for Christians who take their faith seriously. In this case it is a sign of religious growth. A person who is faithful in prayer usually experiences some kind of "dark night of the senses," a period in which the emotional and cultural props of devotion to God simply give way. No longer does it "feel good" to pray, go to church or live a virtuous life. Perseverance in the faith and in prayer often leads into an even bleaker "dark night of the soul," characterized by doubts about God and despair of one's own capacity to continue in God's presence.

The classic works of Christian spirituality have always explained this condition as a necessary prelude to a "transforming union" with God. God prepares us for this kind of union by purifying us from attachments to sin and even by weaning us from our of attachment to our favorite religious feelings and images of the Divine. God in this way enables us to seek only himself rather than our preferred spiritual "props."

Another source of this winter of the spirit is a struggle with God, like Janet's, which ends in telling God to "take it all." Whatever its source, dealing with this dark night of the spirit requires a spiritual maturity that is in somewhat short supply in our warm-fuzzy culture.

When a Christian has sufficient maturity to struggle with God, that means the person does not take God lightly. Someone can believe in God, even profess to be a Christian, and never come to grips with God in a deeply personal way. Struggle is a very personal act. Anyone who contends with God begins to get some idea of who God really is. The subsequent act of surrender to God in all areas of one's being is not to be done frivolously—for the simple reason that God might take us up on our offer. The pattern for this, as for all else in the Christian life, is Jesus himself.

The Spiritual Desolation of Jesus

Jesus, confronted with the suffering and death he would undergo the next day, prayed, "Father, if you are willing, remove this cup from me; yet, not my will but yours be done" (Luke 22:42). Whenever we say the Lord's Prayer, we echo this prayer of Jesus with the words "Thy will be done." Truthfully, we usually don't pay attention to these words or utter them seriously when we say them. Everybody knows the Lord's Prayer, and we say it from memory and unreflectively most of the time.

But if we put enough pieces of the gospel together, we remember that Jesus talked about such things as taking up our cross and following him, the servant not being greater than the master, the grain of wheat needing to die—Jesus said all sorts of things that make us uncomfortable. When we connect these statements and Jesus' own example with his prayer the night before he died (and the words we say so often), "Thy will be done," the picture becomes clearer—and rather stark.

Having understood this dimension of the gospel, one quite rightly struggles with it—Jesus did. When he prayed on the night before he died, "his sweat became like great drops of blood falling down on the ground" (Luke 22:44). When one grasps the significance of this connection, truly struggles with it to the point of some inner "bloody sweat," and then, aware to some extent of what it means, freely and voluntarily tells God to "take it all," one experiences more deeply what Paul meant when he called us to be "conformed to Christ."

Thus the spiritual desolation Janet felt within herself fundamentally relates to the final agony of Jesus. I believe the most enigmatic and poignant statement in the New Testament is the one uttered by Jesus as death approached. Matthew reports, "About three o'clock Jesus cried out with a loud voice . . . 'My God, my God, why have you forsaken me?' " (Matthew 27:46). His cry is actually the first line of Psalm 22, which Jesus would have known by memory from start to finish. Some might argue that Jesus was merely quoting an appropriate psalm. But that misses the point. The cry of the psalmist was genuine. Certainly Jesus' sense of desolation was authentic. It expressed his state of soul as he felt death approach. For Jesus, in his last painful moments, God seemed far away. He felt abandoned by his Father. This is real suffering—nothing about the cross is a sham. Matthew tells us that after his cry of desolation, Jesus cried out once again in a loud voice and "breathed his last" (27:50).

This cry of anguish came from Jesus at the very moment when he was accomplishing our salvation. It was the moment for which he had come into the world. He had done the Father's will perfectly. And yet intimately connected to that moment for Jesus—and for us—was the cry "My God, my God, why have you forsaken me?" This is the biblical source of what Janet experienced within herself. She was called by Jesus to enter more fully into his sufferings in her own interior life.

To feel at some times and at very deep levels "forsaken" by God is thus a part of the Christian experience—though it is not much talked about in our culture, where everything must be as upbeat as possible and knowing God is supposed to make us feel good. Jesus did not "have a nice day" on the cross, and there are times when we— the servants who are not greater than the Master—will share this experience of forsakenness with him.

To "Complete What Is Lacking . . ."

The Christian life—which is really the following of Jesus—is thus intimately involved with his suffering on the cross. This is not just a doctrine to be believed or a set of behaviors to be acted upon; it is an internal reality—something that is reflected in the inner struggles and the prayer of Christians. No one knew this better than Paul, who proclaimed not only by word but by example "Christ crucified" (1 Corinthians 1:23). He knew what it meant to follow Jesus in this way.

But Paul went further than this, rejoicing even in his sufferings because "in my flesh I am completing what is lacking in Christ's afflictions for the sake of his body, that is, the church" (Colossians 1:24). Paul also tells us, "Be imitators of me, as I am of Christ" (1 Corinthians 11:1). Thus the Christian who voluntarily follows Jesus along the way of the cross not only proclaims Christ crucified but in a sense "completes" that suffering for the sake of the Church.

The connection between suffering and the mission of Christ in the world is spelled out further in Acts, again with reference to Paul. Having just encountered the risen Christ on the road to Damascus, Saul of Tarsus is immediately converted. The Lord then appears to Ananias, a disciple in Damascus, and tells him to go to Saul. Ananias objects, but the Lord tells him: "Go, for he is an instrument whom I have chosen to bring my name before Gentiles and kings and before the people of Israel; I myself will show him how much he must suffer for the sake of my name" (Acts 9:15-16).

The rest of Paul's life, his entire vocation, is summed up in this short passage. He is God's chosen instrument. His mission is made quite specific: he is called to carry the name of Jesus out into a very troubled and hostile empire. The final component of his new life as an apostle of Christ, suffering for the sake of Jesus' name, is integrally connected to his calling.

Paul's role in proclaiming the gospel is, of course, crucial and decisive for all time, but his life and mission are also paradigmatic, providing a pattern for subsequent Christian history. His life is an example for us all. Paul's struggles are well documented and remain in the public record of the Church. It is abundantly clear from his own writing that the source of his affliction is not only the opposition he encounters and the disasters that overtake him, but internal as well. Paul sees his own weakness and inadequacy; he ponders his inability to do the good that he wishes to do and avoid the evil that he wishes to avoid. He entreats God to remove his weakness from him, but is told that God's grace is sufficient.

It is clear from his writings that Paul had an intimate, experiential knowledge of the sufferings of Jesus—and that experience is the source of his greatness. He spent much of his life in "the cloud." Christians down through the ages have learned from him.

But Paul never ends with the cross, with the suffering and death of Jesus. He is primarily a witness to the risen Christ. He always sees beyond suffering and death, beyond the sin and sorrow in the world, beyond his own afflictions. Paul not only writes about the new life in the risen Christ, he experiences it. Whatever the troubles, of mind, body, spirit, external circumstances, Paul is able to say: "Rejoice in the Lord always; again I will say, Rejoice. . . . And the peace of God, which surpasses all understanding, will guard your hearts and your minds in Christ Jesus" (Philippians 4:4-7).

Like Paul, the Christian must be about the business of Jesus, reconciling, serving others, confronting the evil powers of the world, living and proclaiming the gospel. But Jesus did not emerge victorious by overpowering the forces of evil. He first underwent suffering and death—to the dismay and scandal of his friends. Only then did God give the final answer in the resurrection. In this way the world is redeemed, transformed and changed. The old saying is still true: "Without the cross there is no crown."

The radical Christians of Generation X, who live almost twenty centuries after the events related in New Testament, are not among the original witnesses to the risen Christ, but they may take to heart what the risen Lord said to Thomas: "Blessed are those who have not seen and yet have come to believe" (John 20:29). Unless they, like those original disciples, experience in some deeply interior way the death of Jesus, they cannot proclaim his resurrection. But as more and more of them are being called to walk with him to the cross, their proclamation is already becoming more powerful.

The Night and the Cloud

There are two metaphors I have found useful in helping Xers who have experiences similar to Janet's. Both are from classic works of Christian spirituality which have stood the test of centuries.

The experience of spiritual desolation is sometimes described as the "dark night of the soul." In this metaphor the first part of the experience resembles twilight, when objects begin to fade from view— this is the period when we begin to anticipate the suffering of the cross. The second part is the very darkness of midnight—we now stand at the foot of the cross and experience something of the suffering of Jesus. We do not at this time see the light. We walk purely by faith. We know that dawn will come, but we see no evidence of it. The third part of the experience comes just before first light. The dawn has not yet arrived, but we can distinguish the surrounding terrain once again. We actually are living in the light during this part of the night—this is the first Easter glimpse of the risen Lord.[2]

I believe this metaphor is most appropriate for Generation X and for our time. Notice how the sense of light played such a part in Janet's experience. Xers are struggling with a generational dark night of the spirit—but if they walk in faith within that night, they begin to experience the glimmer that precedes first light. The radical Christians of Generation X are thus able to speak confidently of dawn at Easter and the light of the risen Christ, because God has already illumined their hearts with a very bright light.

Another metaphor Janet found helpful in understanding her experience was that of "the cloud." This "cloud" is nothing more than an up-close demonstration given by God of the vast gulf that lies between God and humanity. "My thoughts are not your thoughts, nor are your ways my ways" (Isaiah 55:8).

The cloud experience resembles driving through a thick and impenetrable fog or low cloud. Anyone who has ever driven under these conditions knows that you must slow down and sometimes even stop. The same is true in the spiritual journey. It teaches us to trust God even though we do not and cannot know him now face to face. We do not now know how it is that his justice and mercy will be finally vindicated—but we trust that it will. The cloud is a very deep and personal intuition of this.

Here is some advice on what to do in the cloud that Janet found helpful—as have countless others:

You see nothing and feel nothing but a kind of darkness about your mind, as it were, a cloud of unknowing.

You will feel nothing and know nothing except a naked intent toward God in the depths of your being. Try as you might, this darkness and this cloud will remain between you and your God. You will feel frustrated for your mind will be unable to grasp him and your heart will not relish the delight of his love. But learn to be at home in this darkness. Return to it as often as you can, letting your spirit cry out to him whom you love. For if, in this life, you hope to see and feel God as he is in himself it must be within this darkness and this cloud. . . . God in his goodness will bring you to a deeper experience of himself.[3]

A great many committed young Christians encounter the cobwebs and dark places within themselves as Janet did. They too struggle with how much of themselves to surrender to God. I have heard many Xer stories like Janet's and seen the same bewilderment about what is happening to them. Invariably there is immense relief to find that they are not alone in their struggles with themselves and with God. Nor is there anything "wrong" about the changes taking place in their spiritual lives as they enter into their own dark night and experience the cloud for the first time. When they hear the classic religious language applied to themselves, they understand that God is simply calling them into a deeper relationship with him. For this language speaks to them as deeply as it did to the saints and mystics of ages past.

Avoiding Misconceptions

In this experience there are several misconceptions to be avoided. The first is that committing oneself to God in this way frees one from sinfulness and weakness. Nothing could be further from the truth. Janet's description of the light shining into the dusty, dark and cobwebbed corners of her life and of feeling ugly and dirty is a depiction that anyone with a similar experience would understand—it is, in fact, a kind of "bottom line" of Christianity.

We are weak and sinful people. The light of God's presence exposes this truth about ourselves. We can no longer deny it. As it is exposed, we learn to depend on God and not on ourselves. Paul's letters, especially Galatians and Romans, make this very clear. Paul's descriptions are quite accurate portrayals of what goes on in all of us: God's light, beamed into these corners, allows us to see what is really there. This is not a morbid, guilt-ridden experience. Quite the contrary: it is most liberating, for we learn the truth about ourselves and about the lovingkindness of God. We can, perhaps for the first time, really relax spiritually and bask unafraid in God's presence. The Christians of Generation X are quite aware of sin.

The second misconception is one that we must all take to heart as people who have grown up after Freud. The terms that are traditionally used to describe this kind of religious experience—*cloud, dark night of the soul, spiritual desolation* and the like—as well as the self-descriptive "cobwebby" images such as the ones Janet used, must never be confused with psychological language. The dark night and the cloud have nothing to do with lack of self-esteem, feelings of guilt, the residue of trauma, abuse or any particular emotional state. Nor do they have anything to do with depression, anxiety or any other particular kind of feeling. They are related more to cognitive awareness than to emotion. One can be feeling quite good about oneself and one's life and still feel abandoned by God, or one can be in the midst of the cloud and be very much aware of one's own sinfulness. Conversely, one can be in the midst of depression and have no corresponding spiritual sense of cloud or sinfulness. Or one can be emotionally afflicted with the residue of serious abuse, for example, and *also* have a dark night experience. There is simply no direct correlation between emotional states and the content of these spiritual experiences.

I discussed earlier both the prevalent emotional disorders and the questions of meaning that arise in a highly traumatized generation of young adults. I noted that the difficulties in discerning meaning are related to, but are not the same as, the emotional disturbances. Terms like *cloud* and *dark night* used in connection with spiritual experience connote a disruption in the field of meaning—one that is "healthy" in a spiritual sense.

Because of the widespread sense of alienation among Xers, some of which results from the high incidence of trauma, there is a generational search for meaning in the midst of a seemingly pointless existence. The disjuncture between the absence of meaning and the need for it creates in Xers what I believe is a special affinity for the dark night or cloud experience. Given this generational propensity, the "God space" of so many of them is empty in a particular way that seems to incline them toward the cloud.

A third misconception is that interior religious experience of the kind we have been discussing somehow removes a person from service to the world. It does not. It makes one more aware that God is in Christ reconciling the world to himself. Radical Christians of every generation are the first to recall that Jesus told us to feed the hungry, give drink to the thirsty, visit the imprisoned and the like. We are told to "seek the kingdom of God," not to seek ourselves. "Take it all" religious experience leads to the God-given impulse to serve others.

Radical Christians are very busy in the world. The radical Christians of Generation X find themselves in a world that aches for their presence.

A fourth misconception is that a profound, intense experience of God's cleansing the soul is somehow a final and definitive interior housecleaning. It most certainly is not. A person must be open to repeated cleansings—and often the later ones are more painful than the first.

I remember very well, as a young novice in my religious community, hearing the novice master tell us that we were very eager, enthusiastic young Christians and that we doubtless thought God would clean us up and make us holy overnight. He told us that this would be God's work within us throughout our entire lives. As we got older, we would continue to be amazed at how resistant we were to grace. He also told us that our great struggle would be with spiritual pride—an exaggerated sense of our own spiritual condition. I didn't believe him at the time, but I know now that he was right. I can assure you, the cobwebs and the dark, dirty places in the soul endure and even seem to multiply—I continue to uncover new layers within myself all the time. But that's fine, because in this way we begin to understand, as the years pass, that it is truly God at work within us. It is God's strength that makes perfect our weakness.

So the "take it all" Christians of Generation X, who have made so marvelous a commitment in youth, must never be discouraged but continue to be open throughout life to the divine light that exposes and cleans the cobwebs. It is also very important never to pass judgment on the spiritual condition of anyone else or to make comparisons between oneself and another. Youth tends to be intolerant of the spiritual flaws of others. But the only prayer of comparison Jesus tolerates is "Lord, be merciful to me, a sinner."

In order to enhance the cleansing process and to battle the ever-present danger of spiritual pride, it is a good idea to have a "soul friend" or spiritual guide—either an older person or another Xer who is a serious Christian—and to be quite honest and frank about oneself, allowing the other to point out areas of self-deception, hypocrisy and pride. We always miss things in ourselves that others see. The spiritual friend or guide should also be undergoing the same kind of process with someone else. No one can lead in this area without also being led. God allows us in this way to be servants one to another even in our interior lives.

A fifth misconception has to do with emotional states. Awareness of sinfulness has nothing to do with self-esteem or the lack of it. It is simply awareness of who one is in relation to God.

A final misconception is that intense experiences of the kind we have been discussing should be the norm for our subsequent prayer life. They should not be. Most of our experience with God is—and should be—quite ordinary. Even the intense experiences are not necessarily very emotional—they are more a heightened awareness of God's presence and a changed attitude.

We should, in fact, never seek any kind of religious experience— we should only seek God and what God wills for us. Remember that Peter, James and John wanted to remain on the mount of transfiguration and bask in the intense glory of the Lord. Jesus thought otherwise; he brought them down from the mountaintop to continue with him on the road to the cross.

The Christian is—and should be—immersed in the ordinariness of life. For Generation X, life is all about studies, work, dating, avoiding gang violence and drive-by shootings, working out past traumas, being with family and friends, falling in love, finding a career and all the things we do. This is the stuff of life—and of prayer.

Prayer is often distracted, disjointed and desperate. We often don't feel like praying—or going to school or work or being nice to people, or . . . But God is with us in all the ordinary stuff of life. "The Word became flesh and lived among us," and Word-Made-Flesh remains with us in all that we do. The cobwebs and dirty corners of our souls are still there, and the light continues to shine even when we are unaware of its presence. "Take it all" Christians know that God has already taken it all—cobwebs and dirt included.

We are always to some extent in the "cloud" and in the "dark night of the soul." But committed Christians don't worry about it; they just get back to the business of ordinary living and praying, confident that God is always with them. So the radical Christians of Generation X simply go about being tough-minded, tenderhearted, pragmatic, skeptical young adults wearing Levis and T-shirts, or suits and dresses if they must, listening to rock music, sending E-mail and whatever else they do. But these radical Christians are a different kind of Xer.

An Xer Prototype

I want to propose a biblical model for Generation X. Her greatness has been dimmed somewhat in recent centuries, perhaps because she was a woman: Mary Magdalene. Mary was a friend of Jesus and faithful to the end. Unlike all the male disciples except John, she did not flee at the first sign of trouble. She was apparently a very determined person. She stood at the foot of the cross and witnessed the slow, agonizing, brutal death of the One she had come to believe was the long-awaited Messiah. She did not try to evade the fear, the despair and even the possible danger to herself entailed in standing near him.

Xers have a spiritual capacity to relate to the cross, because they already have some experience of the agonizing death of hope. Radical Christians turn intentionally and deliberately to the cross, placing there the death of hope—and then they wait. This is exactly what Mary did. She would not leave, she would not surrender to despair. She waited until the end.

On the first day of the week, she went to the tomb to anoint the body. She saw Jesus, but she did not recognize him. Thinking that he was the gardener, she asked where he had taken the body. He then called her by name: "Mary." In that instant she recognized him and responded. He told her, "Do not hold on to me, because I have not yet ascended to the Father." Jesus then commissioned her to tell the others that he had risen from the dead. Mary did as she was told (John 20:11-18).

Xers wander in the tombs of our culture looking for Jesus, without recognizing him. When the search becomes intentional, they begin to ask the question "Where is he?" The answer comes, as it did for Mary, simply and through a single word. He calls each by name. The radical Christians of Generation X who, like Mary, have the grit and determination to stand by the cross, understand why it is they cannot hold on to him but must go instead and tell others what they have experienced.

Mary Magdalene appears in the biblical story as a person sensitive enough to be a close friend of Jesus. She is also a person of grit and determination—something of what we might call today "toughness," for she "sticks it out." But she responds immediately to that most intimate and personal utterance of her name. I see a resonance between this woman of long ago and the hardy yet sensitive "take it all" folk of Generation X. Above all, they are bonded with Mary Magdalene across the centuries by a message inscribed within their hearts that must still be announced today: "The Lord is risen."

9

A REASON
FOR HOPE

The Blessedness of Generation X (Janet and Bill)

We began this book with what seemed like a lot of "gloom and doom," enumerating the ways in which Generation X has come into young adult maturity in a cultural and moral "whirlwind of barbarism." We have been unsparing in our description of the wasteland that Generation X has inherited. We have talked about broken homes, sexual abuse, economic decline, ecological problems, political ineptitude. We have examined the impact on the young of moral decay in a society permeated with greed. During the months this book has been in preparation, we have seen even further economic decline and evidence of continuing moral erosion. We have indicted the American Church not only for being uninterested in Generation X but, even worse, for being shallow. We have examined the reasons for loss of hope and lack of faith among Xers. We have even titled our book about Xers *A Generation Alone*.

In spite of these enormous problems and afflictions, in spite of the conditions we find prevalent among young adults, we are very hopeful. We are hopeful precisely *because* of what we find among young adults. We believe X is a pivotal generation, perched at the leading edge of a great historical divide between the modern and postmodern eras. We believe X is a generation of pioneers who will be privileged to stamp their imprint on the shape of civilization far into the future.

We believe that the characteristics for which Generation X has received such bad press are the very qualities that will render them most effective as pioneers. Their pragmatism and skepticism, their sharp-eyed assessments of life and, above all, their search for community and personal relationships are exactly what the emerging era requires. Though Xers show no grandiose signs of wanting to "change the world," they will in fact do so in the unobtrusive but significant ways we have mentioned.

We believe, as we have said, that Xers have a "God space" that cries out to be filled. We have said that they are "halfway to the gospel," and we see signs that God is leading them in ever greater numbers and in ever deepening ways into the fullness of the gospel promise.

We have come up with no specific programs or solutions to the cultural, moral and economic problems that we see. To do so would be arrogant and foolish—and would be unfaithful to the spirit of Generation X, which always eschews the grandiose. But we know enough about history to realize that the solutions and answers that are even now fermenting and being tried in quiet, tentative fashion among young adults will be effective on a much larger scale as events unfold.

We are Christians, and we believe beyond all else that our hope lies in a loving Father who is present among us, reconciling us and restoring all things in his Son Jesus our Lord, and who sends the Spirit to move among us and within us—and who moves especially now among those we have termed "a generation alone."

We believe their aloneness is, on the one hand, an impoverishment resembling alienation. But aloneness is a different matter when it becomes a place from which to lift one's soul to seek community and to bear one another's burdens. Aloneness is empowerment and grace when it cries out to God to fill the empty spaces in the soul. Aloneness is a strength because it can become a place of real solitude wherein one can hear the subtle whisperings of God. Aloneness is the springboard from which members of a "lost" generation, having been transformed by God, can open their hearts and hands, inviting others to partake of the gifts they have received. And so it is with Generation X.

A Letter to Generation X (Janet)

Our generation has done a lot of Boomer bashing. We tend to blame them for leading us, with great fanfare, down a path that leads to nowhere. In reality, the Boomers were responding to a wave of cultural change that began before they were even born, and now all generations are realizing the same thing today, but we are realizing it at different stages in our lives.

We are realizing that acquiring more and more *things* leads simply to having more things. It does not result in happiness, or love, or a feeling of security, as we honestly believed it would. The confusion in our world today is due to the fact that we had all been told that we would be happy if we attained certain standards, and we're not.

The Boomers are realizing that the path they have been following leads to nowhere, but they are far, far down the path already and don't know where to turn. The Xers are standing at the beginning of the path, and we can see the confusion and disillusionment of those who have gone before us. We are gradually crowding the opening of the path as we stand around, wondering which way to go, seeing that our only known path leads nowhere. Generations younger than us can't even see a path, and no one knows quite what to tell them about which direction they should take if they are to find a prosperous, purposeful, enjoyable future. Older generations can't understand what happened to the path, because it seemed to work fine for them.

So it has been left up to Generation X to beat a new path. This involves so many crucial questions that at times it is paralyzing! We are being relied upon to create new roles, set new standards and develop new cultural norms. In the past such sweeping changes took decades to develop, yet we are understanding now that we must develop them before we can go anywhere. Where do we begin? Do we have the right tools? Why us? We are the bruised, battered and abandoned generation, right? How can we be expected to be cultural pioneers?

Like the American pioneers who moved west in the nineteenth century, we must also band together, choose a direction and forge our way into new territory. It will be a difficult journey, but we will open a route for others to follow. Those who follow will begin life and live life in a different way from what we have known—in a way, we believe, that will be less hostile and more "we-centered," embodying cultural norms and standards of equality and companionship.

As we stand at the entrance to the well-traveled path, we are beginning to choose our priorities, take stock of our strengths and send out scouts in search of a new direction. We have been criticized repeatedly for not moving. Our detractors have said we aren't dropping out, we aren't following the path, and we aren't going anywhere new. But if they were to step closer, they would see a flurry of activity. They would see a mass of people gathering closer together, planning, taking stock and thinking about how best to lead those who will follow them.

We are just now beginning to move. Generation X has realized that the reason our world seems a hopeless, valueless place is extreme individualism and selfishness. In order to avoid taking yet another dead-end path, we must serve others and we must work together. This requires trust and a lifetime of going against entrenched cultural norms, and it will involve a lot of fear, frustration and anger along the way. But the joy in living again in kindness, friendship and mutual support will be well worth the work it will take to be cultural pioneers.

With love and hope,

Janet

A Letter to Xers and Their Friends (Bill)

I have come to know and love the young adults with whom I have been privileged to work as chaplain and pastor—that much should be clear to anyone who reads this book. I am not uncritical of them. I see their faults, as they see mine. But I enjoy them immensely.

As a Christian, I know that all good things come from God, and I am quite aware of the Spirit of God's movement among us. I know that this God is "ever ancient" but at the same time "ever new." This newness, consonant in every way with the best of what has gone before, is most refreshing. Even now I see God raising up in another generation young men and women with all kinds of gifts. Some among them will certainly be able to fill the shoes of the spiritual giants of our Christian past.

I have a suggestion for older readers, especially those who don't care much for these troublesome young adults: Find some Xers—at work, in the neighborhood, at church. Get to know them, become involved in projects with them, share with them whatever benefits of age and experience you have to offer, but learn from them as well. Enter into real community with them. Be aware of who they really are, show them respect—and, above all, cherish them with great affection. Allow yourself to catch that sacramental glimpse of God in them, and let them see the same in you. And, together with them, "relax and enjoy."

Finally, to our Xer readers: I have been very deeply touched and moved and changed by the members of your generation with whom I have spent much of my time—especially by the "take it all" radical Christians of Generation X. For me, being with you is joyful in the full biblical sense—which means it is fun and laughter-filled as well. I rejoice in you.

To let Paul have the last word: "Again I will say, Rejoice."

With love and hope,

Bill

Notes

Chapter 1: Aloneness

[1]*The Diagnostic and Statistical Manual of Mental Disorders,* 3rd ed., rev. (Washington, D.C.: American Psychiatric Association, 1987). DSM III-R, as this work is known, is the basic manual for psychiatrists and other mental health professionals. It contains diagnostic categories and descriptions of symptoms. Posttraumatic stress disorder' is DSM III-R number 309.89, pp. 247-50.

[2]I know several psychiatrists, specialists in PTSD, who are at the time of this writing preparing papers for publication on this issue. Their opinion is that PTSD cannot be treated effectively unless the religious and moral questions are considered in the treatment process. I have participated as an invited speaker on this topic in at least six conferences of mental health professionals during the two-year period prior to writing this book. There is no longer much doubt that PTSD treatment must deal with moral and religious issues.

[3]Borderline personality disorder, DSM III-R 301.83, pp. 346-47. Borderline personality is a "marked and persistent identity disturbance. This is often pervasive and is manifested by uncertainty about . . . self-image, sexual orientation, long-term goals or career choice, types of friends or lovers to have, or which values to adopt. The person often experiences this instability of self-image as chronic feelings of emptiness or boredom."

[4]Richard Chessick, *Intensive Psychotherapy of the Borderline Patient* (New York: Jason Aronson, 1977), p. 23.

[5]Ibid., pp. 24-26.

[6]William Strauss and Neil Howe, *Generations* (New York: Morrow, 1991), pp. 324-28. See also a Center for Disease Control study reported in Marlene Cimons, "Study Shows a Million Teen Suicides," *Los Angeles Times,* September 20, 1991.

Chapter 2: Generation X

[1]Strauss and Howe, *Generations,* pp. 69-110.

[2]Aaron Bernstein et al., "What Happened to the American Dream: Is Uncle Sam Short-changing Young Americans?" *Business Week,* August 19, 1992.

[3]Congressional Budget Office statistics released in December 1991, based on 1990 census data. Reported in Sylvia Nasar, "The 1980's: A Very Good Time for the Rich," *The New York Times,* March 5, 1992, p. 1. Representative Bernard Sanders, the lone member of the U.S. House of Representatives from Vermont, reports substantially the same figures in "Whither American Democracy?" *Los Angeles Times,* January 16, 1992, p. B1.

[4]Donald L. Barlett and James B. Steele, *America: What Went Wrong* (Kansas City, Mo.: Andrews and McMeel, 1992), esp. prologue and chap. 1. See also William Greider, *Who Will Tell the People? The Betrayal of American Democracy* (New York: Simon & Schuster, 1992), esp. chap. 9; and Donald L. Barlett and James B. Steele, "Caught in the Crunch," *San Diego Union,* November 17, 1991, p. A1.

[5]Barbara Dafoe Whitehead, "Dan Quayle Was Right," *The Atlantic* 271 (April 1993): 47.

[6]James Patterson and Peter Kim, *The Day America Told the Truth* (New York: Prentice Hall, 1991). This book is simply a report of a survey taken of American attitudes about morality. The authors themselves were surprised and chagrined by their findings. The entire book is a somber commentary on the deteriorated state of American morality.

[7]Glenn Tinder, *The Political Meaning of Christianity* (Baton Rouge: Louisiana State University Press, 1989). The thesis of this excellent book is that we can't be good without God. This is a tightly reasoned argument that secularism simply cannot sustain a moral culture. A brief synopsis of the book was published in *The Atlantic* 264 (December 1989) under the title "Can We Be Good Without God?"

Chapter 3: The God Space

[1]Robert Kuttner, in "Jellyfish Economy," *San Diego Union,* May 31, 1993, uses such terms as *spineless* and *invertebrate* to describe the economy. These images are equally apt to describe the prevailing moral and religious conditions of our society.

[2]Unfortunately, I have not been able to find the original source for the term "the Imperial Self."

Chapter 4: The Healing Community

[1]DSM III 309.89.

[2]Ibid.

[3]DSM III 301.83.

[4]Ibid.

[5]Michael H. Stone, "The Fate of Borderline Patients," *Harvard Mental Health,* March 1992, p. 2.

[6]DSM III 313.82.

[7]Peter Marin, "Living in Moral Pain," *Psychology Today,* November 1980, p. 80.

[8]Viktor Frankl, *Man's Search for Meaning* (New York: Washington Square, 1963), p. 154.
[9]See Landy F. Sparr, M. J. Maxwell, J. F. Ferguesson and W. P. Mahedy, "Reassessing Psychic Trauma: Moral Dimensions," *CME Syllabus: American Academy of Psychiatry and Law,* October 21-24, 1993, p. 82.

Chapter 5: Personal Relationships
[1]W. E. Vine, *An Expository Dictionary of New Testament Words* (Old Tappan, N.J.: Revell, 1966), p. 97.

Chapter 6: Changing the World
[1]Tinder, *Political Meaning of Christianity.*

Chapter 7: The Church
[1]Robert N. Bellah et al., *Habits of the Heart: Individualism and Commitment in American Life* (Berkeley: University of California Press, 1985), p. 239.
[2]We let this statement stand without documentation because the controversy isn't really relevant to most Xers. It seems clear that the Xer Church will afford women an equal place of leadership at all levels. Good biblical scholarship increasingly demonstrates that this is not in conflict with Scripture. An excellent book in this regard is John Temple Bristow, *What Paul Really Said About Women: An Apostle's Liberating Views on Equality in Marriage, Leadership and Love* (San Francisco: HarperCollins, 1991).
[3]Charles M. Olsen, "The Closet, the House and the Sanctuary," *The Christian Century,* December 9, 1981.

Chapter 8: Take It All
[1]*Webster's Encyclopedic Unabridged Dictionary of the English Language* (New York: Outlet Book, 1989).
[2]John of the Cross, *The Ascent of Mount Carmel,* in *The Collected Works of St. John of the Cross,* ed. Kieran Kavanaugh and Otilio Rodriguez (Washington, D.C.: Institute of Carmelite Studies, 1979), p. 109.
[3]*The Cloud of Unknowing,* ed. William Johnston (Garden City, N.Y.: Image/Doubleday, 1973), pp. 48-49.